EXPLORING THE "ZONE"

EXPLORING THE "Zone"

By Larry Miller
with James Redfield

PELICAN PUBLISHING COMPANY
Gretna 2001

*The word "Pelican" and the depiction of a pelican are trademarks
of Pelican Publishing Company, Inc., and are registered in the
U.S. Patent and Trademark Office.*

Library of Congress Cataloging-in-Publication Data

Miller, Larry, 1947-
    Exploring the "zone" / by Larry Miller with James Redfield.
        p. cm.
    ISBN 1-56554-717-9 (alk. paper)
    1. Success—Psychic aspects. 2. Mind and body. 3. Supernatural.
4. Human evolution—Miscellanea. I. Redfield, James. II. Title.

BF1045.S83 .M55 2000
131—dc21   00-038531

Printed in the United States of America

Published by Pelican Publishing Company, Inc.
1000 Burmaster Street, Gretna, Louisiana 70053

Contents

Part of the proceeds from
this book will go to *The Farm,*
in honor of
A. L. Staveley and
G. I. Gurdjieff.

Foreword

Of all the terms being used in sports today, one of the newest and fastest-growing expressions is "the zone." You hear it everywhere—on the track among runners, on tennis and racquetball courts, and especially in golf. Whether among professionals on television, with our weekly foursomes, or on the practice range with juniors, the term "zone" is used more and more to describe that special state of mind that exists when one's game spontaneously clicks in, becomes effortless, and rises to a new level of effectiveness.

In reality, of course, this state of functioning is not confined to just sports. It can happen during any focused activity: driving, public speaking, teaching, surgery, in sales—anything we might be doing where our skills and intent suddenly become more effortless and "on" than usual. In years past, "the ability to concentrate and focus" was the phrase that came closest to describing the zone feeling. You would hear sports commentators say this to describe someone who was doing especially well on a particular day. Yet all along, those who experienced this kind of peak moment knew that those old descriptions really didn't adequately describe what was happening. During these special times, the "same old us" (with the same old ability) somehow leaped to a new level of competence, at least for a little while, so we knew that a lot more was there than we knew how to talk about. With the use of the term "zone," we now seem to be bringing this experience more fully into public discourse and understanding.

I believe there is already much agreement emerging on the details of how this experience feels. Not only does our *ability* shift, but also our sense of "who we are" changes. Our awareness moves from a piecemeal focus, jumping sequentially along the many parts of the activity, to a broader, more holistic view of what we are doing. For example, in golf, we might move from a state where we are trying to remember to keep our arm straight, stay down, and shift our weight, to a state of mind where we just "know" how to swing the club back. During the zone state, the details of what we are doing begin to happen automatically, not from conscious ego, but from a larger sense of self that has greater awareness and confidence and knows how to perform the zone activity without thinking. In this book, Larry Miller thoroughly explores this mysterious experience, eloquently describing it in deep descriptions of modern psychology and relating it to several, more esoteric traditions that lend additional perspective. Most helpful of all, he describes various practical techniques that have been shown to help us all move into the zone experience more often.

In many ways, we are all witnessing a step in human evolution taking place before our eyes. For many centuries, we in the West have suffered from the illusion that all of us live in the same state of awareness and level of functioning all the time. Now, thankfully, a new insight is occurring, one in which we are ready to explore and utilize higher mental experiences. Behind the door of awareness lies a glimpse of our full potential.

Larry's book is helping to open that door.

JAMES REDFIELD
Author of *The Celestine Prophecy*
and *The Secret of Shambhala*

Acknowledgments

Some say that the teaching dies with the teacher, that his message is only for *his* time. It is not so. There is a Sufi word—"baraka"—that means an impalpable force imparted by masters to people, places, and situations. This intangible force can be imparted with specific effects that appear when appropriate. It works on the pupil according to the time, place, need—and the circumstances in which he finds himself.

The baraka, for instance, can be imparted to the student as he reads prescribed texts, even though he may feel that he is absorbing very little. The baraka will filter through to his being and collect as a substance in a special reservoir to be drawn upon when needed. And so it is with my teacher, G. I. Gurdjieff, who died in 1949. His teachings bubble to the surface every day from the depths of my consciousness, sometimes when least expected. So I acknowledge him for teaching me magic, magnetism, hypnotism, and alchemy and for showing me how to develop a soul. I acknowledge him *for watering my seeds* and for answering *all* of my questions.

On a more current level I wish to acknowledge those closest to me in my personal life, the ones who give of themselves in so many ways: my parents, John G. Miller, Jr. ("Wimpy" to his buddies), and Walterine Eschette Miller ("Peggy"), who have transcended the ordinary concept of unconditional love; and my sons, Ryan John Miller, Jeffrey Lawrence Miller, and Jonathan Goodwin Miller, who inspire me to do the same.

James and Salle Redfield are friends who know how to charge the human battery. They inspire everyone around them, and they fill the space around them with quiet peace and special love.

Tony and Carol Schueler—I'm sure I've known them forever, such is the wordless bond we share, unaffected by space or time. Tony is in no small way very responsible for my completing this work. He serves as an ever-present adviser (and more) and introduced me to the work of Gurdjieff. Tony is a very rare blend: a mystic, a poet, and a creative, successful businessman.

The woman who shares my life—my joys and sorrows—wears so many hats that she's almost unidentifiable. She constantly holds up the mirror, just by her presence, in which I see my reflection when I forget to look for myself. The word for Connie is "consistent," in her integrity, in her loyalty, and in her willingness to help. She is a successful businessperson, an expert sailor, a certified scuba-diving instructor, and a near-scratch champion amateur golfer. Beautiful inside and outside, talented and smart—what a *special lady* she is!

And she greatly contributed to this book, in many, many ways, just as she's done on all the others. Thanks, Connie. I love you.

A special thanks goes to the folks at Pelican Publishing Company. As the writing of this book progressed, I felt an urge to have it published in my own hometown, New Orleans. Somehow, it just *felt* like the thing to do. So much personal history— good and bad, joys and sorrows—is there. And isn't that life?

Dr. Calhoun, the publisher, quietly turns out incredibly beautiful work. His staff is creative, inspirational, and very competent—a terrific combination. My editor, Nina Kooij, kept me in line and on time—a very competent lady. She is truly a pleasure to work with.

Thank you, New Orleans.

Introduction

In *The Celestine Prophecy,* it was revealed that a progression of *insights,* or "revelations," is manifesting throughout the cultures of the world. These insights form a clear path for our spiritual evolution and will eventually lead us to states of higher energy as we move from materialism to spirituality. We will become "lighter" and vibrate at a higher rate.

Already, despite the selective negativity of the news media, we can see the stirrings of this movement—stirrings brought on by love and compassion. For every news story involving crime and hatred, there are thousands of stories of kindness, warmth, and love. But those stories, for the most part, never make the news. If we could lift the veil from the news we see and hear, we'd learn of a different world out there, one that is rapidly changing for the better, due to the evolution of consciousness on planet Earth.

Science now tells us that the world "out there" is *not* a material one, that all matter is energy that is shaped, by density of molecular structure, vibrational frequency, and human imagination, into different forms. Your hand, for instance, is energy, and so is your kitchen table. And although neither is really "solid," you cannot pass your hand through the table because the table's energy is more densely packed—and vibrates at much lower speeds than the energy that is your hand. Your hand's energy is much "lighter" than that of the table.

It is interesting to note that in the histories of religions and certain esoteric disciplines, many saints, ecstatics, shamans, and other "enlightened beings" were reported to exhibit various forms of "lightness." They were often depicted as "floating," being "lighter than air," and many reports of levitation are documented regarding these saints and masters. It seems that these higher states of human energy give rise to this "lightness."

In the modern sports world—and among practitioners of various dancing disciplines, including ballet—many top performers, in describing moments and periods of peak performance, speak of feeling extraordinarily "light on their feet." And in studying the research on extraordinary human functioning, of which Michael Murphy's *The Future of the Body* is the definitive work, and comparing voluminous reports, accounts, and descriptions of people performing at their highest levels of efficiency, many other common denominators can be found.

In recent years a sort of catch phrase has developed describing human performance that greatly transcends the norm. It started in the arena of athletics but has now spread to all areas of activity. Now a household term, this phenomenon is called "the zone," or being "in the zone." Since most people think that "the zone" is just a *random visit of a special grace,* these sudden "hot streaks," these unexpected displays of rare excellence, have taken on an air of great mystery. But we are going to show you quite a different reality.

In this groundbreaking effort of discovery and insight, gleaned from research, study, and personal experiences, this book will show that "the zone," that rare arena of peak human performance, is really a momentary glimpse, a brief attainment, of the higher energies of our spiritual evolution. And we will show that these higher energy states can be cultivated. We can "call them up." In other words, we can *set the stage* for "zone" experiences to occur. We can intentionally align our energies.

Those of us who learn to raise our energies to higher levels will glimpse more often uncharted territories within ourselves. We will become *"evolutionary scouts,"* and we will help to define a new era of human functioning—one where we move toward a world where we all operate at peak efficiency, feeding off of one another's higher functioning through sympathetic resonance as well as human emotion.

So as we begin the new millennium, we consider this the perfect time to share with you our gift, the gift of our discoveries and insights, a gift that will present you with *specific, personalized techniques* for raising your energy, for accelerating your spiritual evolution, for elevating your every performance, *for entering "the zone."* We feel that the new millennium will see us all dramatically expand our *limitless human potential* as we strive, never ending, toward the Absolute. As always, it is the journey itself that furnishes the magic.

Author's note: This book is the result of work and research on the "zone" phenomenon that was undertaken after many discussions with my friend, author James Redfield. In 1996, James and I decided that the definitive work on what is called "the zone" needed to be done. Though not co-authored, this book is a collaborative effort in every sense, and no one who has read James' stunning work could fail to know that he is one of those rare and lucky people who spend a lot of time in that magical place called "the zone." His latest book, *The Secret of Shambhala,* will change your life.

EXPLORING THE "ZONE"

CHAPTER 1

Exploring and Cultivating the Zone State

"The Zone." They've become household words, a catch phrase for moments of peak performance. "She was *in the zone.*" You've heard and read those words a thousand times, most often in the world of athletics. You've probably used the words a few times yourself (but probably not often enough). "The zone" is when things *really start clicking,* sort of an *automatic pilot of elevated performance,* and it can happen during *any* activity, mental or physical.

Poets, when deeply inspired and creating beauty in abundance and with ease, are in "the zone." Great speakers, when they're "on," enter into it. Musicians, when composing, fall into it from time to time, producing timeless classics.

Any duty, however seemingly ordinary, and any activity, however mundane, can give occasional rise to the zone's mysterious appearance, as excellence of performance beyond the norm occurs. And just as quickly and mysteriously, "it" is gone. But these glimpses of our true potential, however brief, keep us coming back.

For most people, getting into the zone is a very infrequent, random happening that just "appears" out of nowhere. And it disappears just as suddenly. For those who accept these special times as some sort of random grace, peak performance will always be rare. But for those who wish to look deeper than surface reality, a fertile field exists, a field where the zone is always available to those who know how to cultivate it. It is within this same field that the world of synchronicity (meaningful coincidences) lies.

The first step to accessing these realms is to become aware of their existence. Only then can we take the steps necessary to become receptive to their world of information. Surface reality, or the *explicate order,* as it is called by quantum physicist David Bohm (protégé of Einstein and one of the main architects of the holographic theory), is blurred by the ego and by the conscious mind with its running thoughts. But the *implicate,* or *hidden, order* is the field of ultimate reality, the realm of *pure awareness.* Sogyal Rinpoche, author of the fabulous classic *The Tibetan Book of Living and Dying,* calls it the *nature of mind,* the *Rigpa.* To G. I. Gurdjieff, it was *essence.* And our only human conscious links to the implicate order, where the reality of our true potential lies, are our *senses.* Pure sensory awareness, untainted and basic, can serve as a pathway to that elusive and mysterious place we call "the zone."

The zone is, as we will see, an alignment of factors, and the main goal of this book is to show that this alignment, while sometimes occurring accidentally, can be one of intentional design. If we know *what* to align, and *how* to align, then we clear the way for our senses to lead us into that state, that place that we call "the zone."

The Ranks of the Efficient

Being "in the zone" has been popularized greatly by the sports media, and, as so often happens with buzzwords and catch phrases, it has taken on an aura much greater and more mysterious than its true nature. The average sports fan considers the zone to be something remote and magical and associates it only with superstars at their best. But in reality, the zone is nothing more than peak efficiency, of which we all are capable. The fact is, we are all superstars, some of us as parents, others as teachers or workers. Whatever our activity, we are all capable of doing our best.

Just imagine a world where everyone performs at his or her best more often, regardless of how trivial and nonessential the activity may seem. In the grand scheme of things, whatever you're doing, *at that moment,* is indeed most important. This has been the ultimate essence of Zen practice for centuries.

Take a moment and think about it. Mentally take yourself through a typical day in your life. Imagine every person that you encounter during the day—every person—performing at his best, operating "in the zone" in his particular field or activity. How would that impact your day and your life? Think of how that would spread out through society—one person at a time feeding off of another's positive energy. We not only know that such a world is possible, we believe that the human culture is moving toward it. Evolution has a way of *eventually* smoothing out the edges. Just witness the universal feature of "roundness."

The value of being able to willfully, quickly enter that elusive state of functioning called "the zone" is incalculable. Every individual, from every imaginable walk of life, could greatly benefit from the ability to "call up" extraordinary states of efficiency, where performance at their higher potentials is available to them. For some, this ability would be life saving in nature—for others, financially rewarding. And for many others, it would add great joy and satisfaction to every facet of their lives. "Bad days" could be stopped in their tracks, arguments and disagreements snuffed out and forgotten before taking their toll on precious human energy. There would be no more "wondering what to do" in confusing situations, and the quandary would be replaced by immediate positive action that would propel the morale to transformational heights.

Most people associate the zone with athletic performance, but elevated states of functioning can and do occur in all human activity. As you read the real-life scenarios below, you will get a better idea of how we all need to "put our best foot forward" more often, in so many important situations. In the overall scheme of things, emergency life-saving surgical technique seems to outweigh the game-winning basket in the playoffs. But many situations in your everyday life cry out for the best that you can give.

The zone does not have to be a random visit by a "special grace." There are definite steps that lead to its emergence from the implicate order of our highest potentials. We are going to show you what the zone is all about and how to access it on demand.

I have spent many years studying, teaching, and practicing the elements of extraordinary human functioning, in the arena of consciousness—its history as well as its future direction—and in the fields of athletic performance and mind-body connection. We know that the zone can be cultivated and coaxed, that its appearance is not reserved for "special" people in certain fields of endeavor. Whichever activity you'd like to optimize performance or enjoyment of, *you can,* and the secret keys are all locked away inside of you. This book will lead you to those keys and show you how to use them to join the "ranks of the efficient."

Dr. Steve Redmond, Heart Surgeon

Dr. Steve Redmond, at forty-six, had reached the pinnacle of his profession. One of the world's most famous and respected heart surgeons, he specialized in intricate, difficult procedures that many other top surgeons would refuse to perform. Steve seemed to thrive on pressure and would seek out these complicated cases as if to present himself with the challenge. But his reasons were not altogether selfish and personal. He had a genuine love of the foundation of his work: to save lives and help humankind. A compassionate and sensitive man, he was the type who would just as soon work for nothing, if it meant restoring an individual's vitality or a family's happiness.

It was February 5, 1997, and Steve was relaxing at his desk in his Houston office, enjoying a rare quiet moment. He was thinking about a conversation several months ago at a cocktail party in honor of his only son's signing of a University of Texas at Austin football scholarship. Steve himself was an avid and talented tennis player, had played collegiately, and had almost tried the professional ranks until prevailed upon by his father to finish medical school. He was glad that he did, for he loved his work, made a lot of money, and still played tennis several times a week. The conversation had revolved around tennis, and in particular that mysterious and elusive state of performance called "the zone."

Steve had had many conversations on this topic in the past—he was friends with several former and current touring tennis professionals, some of whom had been his college teammates. What was particularly interesting to Steve was that his experiences with the zone on the tennis courts mirrored similar experiences in the operating room, when unpredictably he suddenly found himself performing at the very highest levels of his ability, instinctively, as if on some sort of "automatic pilot." As always, the conversation centered around the mystery of the zone's seemingly random appearance, how it "just happens."

Steve's daydreams and recollections were interrupted by a quick knock and a sudden entrance by his longtime office manager, Phyllis. The look on her face and her manner of entry told him that something was very wrong. "Line one, Steve. It's Memorial Hospital in Austin, emergency room."

Picking up the phone on his desk, with Phyllis uncharacteristically *not* leaving the room, Steve had a feeling that his world was about to be shattered. The intuition was accurate. The stone-cold, monotone voice on the other end told him that he should come immediately. His son, Brad, had been struck by a car on campus and the situation was very critical.

Ignoring the pursuit of details, he slammed the receiver down, picked it up again, dialed Fred Watson's private direct number, and waited. Fred was one of Steve's closest friends, his family attorney, and a pilot with a private plane.

Twenty minutes after Fred answered the phone, Steve, his wife, Morgan, and Fred were climbing into the plane. The short flight to Austin featured a silence broken only by the wind and the whirring sound of the engines—and the pounding of three hearts. The car from the hospital was waiting as the plane touched down, and in fifteen minutes the three were rushing through the entrance to the emergency-room area, still stuck in a silence that was about to be broken.

"I'm Dr. Steve Redmond, Brad Redmond's father. Where is my son?"

"Yes, Dr. Redmond, we've been waiting for you," said the head nurse. "He is in room four, with Doctors Wagner and Thomson. They said for me to—"

Her words were cut off by Steve's quick "Thank you" as he and Morgan headed for room four. Fred took a seat in the waiting area, immersed in deep concern for his friend. Doctors Jack Wagner and Jim Thomson greeted Steve and Morgan at the door and gave them a quick summary of the situation. These two doctors were not strangers to Steve. They were two of the best *heart* men around, and Steve had been involved in seminars and consultations with both men over the years. *Heart* men, thought Steve, as Jack Wagner started speaking, dispensing with formalities.

"It's not good, Steve. There have been critical injuries to the heart area, and especially to the heart itself. If not successfully repaired, and quickly, we're not going to be able to save him. Take a look." Holding up the x-rays, the two doctors went on to point out and explain the specific location and nature of the damage.

The second that Steve saw the pictures, a lump formed in his throat and the sweat began. The injuries were monumental and very critical and appeared at first to be insurmountable. But then Steve's training and experience kicked in and he searched for a way. As Morgan left the room sobbing, Steve came to the sudden, paralyzing realization of something that the other two specialists already knew—that Dr. Steve Redmond was the *only* man capable of successfully performing— even attempting—the necessary procedure, one that was unprecedented in the annals of heart surgery. The bottom line was, Steve had to wing it through never-before-performed heart surgery on his own son, and he had to do it now. Steve couldn't afford the luxury of waiting for a "special grace" to visit upon him—he had to access the zone, he had to perform, on immediate demand, at his very highest level.

At times like these, people can think of strange things. There is nothing congruous or predictable about a panicked mind. As Steve hurriedly prepared for surgery, he wondered about his conversations about the zone. Would this be one of those times when extraordinary functioning paid a random visit? Or would the pressure prevail? Desperately, Steve wished that he held the key to entering the zone.

Douglas Walker, High-School Basketball Player

Douglas Walker was gifted. From his earliest days in Little League, he had been the "shining star." Quick and strong, with a phenomenal shooting eye, he had led the team and league in scoring every year, up to and including this, his senior year at Worthington High, one of the Midwest's prep powers in basketball. And not just a showcase of individual talent, he'd led his team to numerous titles with his all-around play—rebounding, dishing out assists, and playing tenacious defense.

There was only one problem, and the college scouts, while drooling over his statistics, were watching the state playoffs with great interest and concern. It had become evident over the years, in a definite repeating pattern, that Douglas was a "choker," able to perform at his best only when unchallenged. It seemed (and Douglas was *very privately* keenly aware of it) that in practice with the team, when shooting alone, or in games when the team had a huge lead, his shooting was at its very best. He seemed, at these times, to easily enter that state called "the zone." At those times, his shots, indeed his every move, seemed flawless. He would sink long shots, dead center, in extended streaks. His jumping seemed more lively and his moves smoother than usual. And it all seemed to happen automatically, as if controlled from somewhere else. But when pressure was present, be it from an equal opponent (or one whose performance was better than normal) or from himself, his performance dropped markedly. Douglas loved to practice shooting alone, for it provided access to the safety and peace of the zone. Sometimes he wondered if there might be a way to access it during times of intense and challenging competition. But he always just finally concluded that it was unexplainable, this mysterious state of perfection that seemed to steal over him.

Douglas came from a family that was by no means affluent, with several brothers and sisters in various stages of schooling. Financial pressures on the family were staggering. And as he approached college and weighed the plethora of scholarship offers on the table, it was becoming obvious that an *extremely* attractive professional contract loomed on the horizon, providing, of course, that he performed in college and continued to receive the extensive national media attention that had been part of his high-school career. But in order for this to happen, Douglas was going to have to impress these college and professional scouts during these state playoffs. He would have to replicate his spectacular season-long performances, and *do it against the other playoff teams.* There was no doubt in anyone's mind about his gifts. But could he display those gifts when it really mattered?

Suiting up for the opening playoff game, with his family, friends, and scouts in the stands, Douglas searched his frantic mind for the key to that special place he'd visited so many times—that place called "the zone."

Evelyn Waters, Artist

Evelyn Waters, internationally known contemporary artist, had hit a snag at the wrong time. Her biggest exhibit of the year, the International Exhibit in Paris, was four months away, and she had been commissioned to produce the entryway showpiece, capturing on canvas the spirit of the contemporary art scene as the world entered the new millennium.

Typical of Evelyn's style was a flood of productivity for weeks and sometimes even months, followed by unexplained periods of no production whatsoever, much like the "blocks" encountered by writers and poets. During the prolific stretches, the work seemed to flow in torrents, with almost no conscious effort or planning. In fact, she sometimes wondered where the inspiration came from—and what triggered its appearance.

Having finally finished all of her promised and committed work, she now turned her full attention to the piece for the International Exhibit. But the problem was, *nothing came.* Knowing that the deadline was quickly approaching, and that she was getting, at best, a very late start, only served to make the situation worse, and the pressure to produce increased as the days raced by.

Near panic, Evelyn sat at her canvas, at the mercy of the Muse, wishing she could somehow entice the brush to stroke. She wondered about those effortless, thoughtless times when the art just oozed out of her, when phenomenal creativity *just happened.* What brought on those times and, more importantly, what could be done to bring it on now? Her reputation was on the line. She *needed to access the zone.*

Melissa Parker, Housewife

Melissa Parker, college educated and multitalented, was happily putting her skills and training to use as a very busy housewife and mother of three young children. Her days were as filled and as hectic as those of any high-powered CEO. Her husband, Ron, was a rising star in a major corporation, and the family had just been transferred as the result of a significant promotion: new city, new and bigger home, new friends—and new bosses.

While trying to adjust to all of the logistical changes and challenges, Melissa was simultaneously handling a daily schedule that left precious few quiet moments. One day at two o'clock, in the middle of considerable mayhem with more timetables than seemed possible to meet, her car phone rang and it was Ron, calling excitedly from the office.

"Honey, I know this is a little 'last minute,' but . . ."

Melissa knew this line and braced for the news that would turn the already unmanageable day into a real challenge.

"Mr. Parsons"—Tom Parsons, Ron's new boss—"and *his* boss, Walter Kennedy, the *national* marketing manager, want to meet you and the kids. So I invited them to dinner. Problem is, Mr. Kennedy leaves in the morning, so it has to be *tonight*. Sorry for the lack of notice, but it just sort of developed in the last half-hour. Can you do it?"

While Ron waited for a reply, Melissa counted to ten. She said, "Of course, no problem. Tell them cocktails at 6:30, dinner at 7:30." And the line went dead, not out of rudeness but necessity. Melissa was the type who loved a challenge, and this more than qualified. The race was on.

On certain days, Melissa noticed, things just sailed along in perfect harmony, no hitches, no missed deadlines. Everything that she did seemed automatically to turn out to be the ideal action required for the moment. And on those days the evening meals that she served were borderline gourmet delights. She thought about this as she pulled into the supermarket parking lot, with no idea at all what she should prepare for this most important meal or, for that matter, how she could even possibly pull it off.

Melissa silently wished for that rare and wonderful state where everything flowed, with almost no conscious thought. She was searching for the zone. How I wish, she thought, that I could just transform myself into that mode, that mode where everything moves along with total efficiency.

Joe Wallace, Sanitation Worker

Joe Wallace worked for Hirsch Industries, a waste-disposal company in a major Midwestern city. Joe was a garbage man. One night, while enjoying a pleasant dinner and a glass of wine with his wife, Jennie, Joe started talking about his job. He was in a great mood, and he wanted to talk. This was a rare event in the Wallace household.

The day had gone extraordinarily well for Joe. His crew had gotten an early start, had encountered no hitches, and had finished an hour and a half early. The weather had been great, and his boss had taken notice of and mentioned the crew's efficiency. This was the kind of day that led to better routes and pay raises. Joe's day had been free of the hassles that had all too often resulted in severe headaches that left him exhausted, grouchy, and silent. There were many evenings that Joe just wasn't much fun to be around. But this was not one of those. Let's pick up the conversation on this special night at the Wallaces'.

"I tell you, Jen, if only every day could be like this one. Everything went so perfectly you wouldn't believe it. No spills, no messes. I even smelled good when I finished. People were actually nice and friendly—even helpful. Today, I *actually enjoyed* being a garbage man."

"Joe, you're a *sanitation worker,* not just a 'garbage man.' And your job is vital to the community."

"Call it what you want, Jennie, but all I do is pick up garbage. But, yes, it is vital. And on days like this one I see that, I look at it that way. But why are days like this *so rare?* Most of the time I hate the job. I look at it as almost a punishment. Most of the time people just throw their garbage out in a mess and expect us to tidy it up for them. *And they're nasty about it!* It blows all over the street, and when we don't pick it all up, which is not possible, they call and complain, and the supervisor calls us in. *We* get docked for *their* sloppiness. Why can't every day be like today, when everything just goes right?"

Even garbage men can get into the zone. You don't have to be in the seventh game of the NBA Finals to have a "peak performance" experience. Little did Joe know that indeed almost every day *could be* like "that day," when things seem to go right all day long. He had no clue that those days did not have to *just happen,* that they could be cultivated and coaxed into reality. Joe's job could indeed become a delight—every day. Any job can. You don't just *get* into the zone. You have to take the necessary steps.

Jason Sellers, Salesman

Jason Sellers, only thirty-two, was already becoming a legend in the world of selling. Employed by an industry-leading corporate giant, he had established new sales records for five years running. Even more remarkable was the fact that he seemed to work fewer hours than anyone else in the company. But Jason had a secret method. While possessing the usual traits typical of great salesmen—charm, good looks, a friendly manner, etc.—he also had a keen intuition about his own ability to "perform."

Jason would wake up two or three days a week and *know* that he was "on." And on those days he would go out and sell *anything* he wanted to *anyone* he wanted. On those days he never failed. On other days he just didn't have the same "feel" about things, and so he'd sleep late, go to the beach, or play tennis—anything but sell.

Some of his co-workers were envious and called him lazy, others called him lucky, but very few saw the wisdom of his philosophy. Aside from his natural gifts, he had this amazing ability to "pick his spots"—to sniff out perfect sales scenarios. And he had the instinctive perception to spend his "down" time rejuvenating his mind and body.

Jason didn't know it, but he was close to unlocking the door that leads to the zone. But "close" wouldn't help him with the dilemma he was about to face. P. Roger Watson was regional sales manager for the company, and he was Jason's boss. Given Jason's phenomenal production, Roger gave him free rein regarding office time, and Jason was a favorite business-lunch companion, especially when entertaining prospective clients.

One day when Jason was in the office, Watson called him in. "Jason, keep lunchtime open this Friday, and then a couple of hours after that. Tom Walker is coming in, and I'd like to take him on a few cold calls with you. He wants to see for himself how you do it. He can hardly believe the numbers. I figure we'll make two or three calls—just enough to dazzle him—and then bring him to the airport. Needless to say, this is rather important. The CEO only visits a regional office a couple of times a year, and it's usually a very short visit. Something like this is unprecedented. You really need to shine."

This was Wednesday—two days' notice. Jason could hardly believe his ears. Performing when *he* felt like performing was one thing, but performing on demand was quite another. And his reputation—not to mention his future with the company— depended on it.

Jason went home that evening, had dinner, and went to bed early. He went to sleep wondering how to wake up Friday morning in his "on" mode. He desperately needed to spend Friday "in the zone."

Recognizing the Zone

A close friend, Tony Schueler of Seattle, Washington, and a near-scratch golfer provides this eloquent description of a higher functioning. "The sign reads, Speed Zone Ahead, and we know to slow down. (What about speeding up?) The question in my mind is the recognition of the zone—be it momentary or sustained, transitory or continuous—and in the rare moments of recognition, what to do about it. Oh, yeah, while in the zone, time does slow down, doesn't it?

"The mark of time . . . perhaps moments in time that have the event itself taking on a focal point in memory well beyond the not so memorable . . . the really 'important' stuff. Is 'the really important stuff' a dedicated thread in the tapestry of our self-image, and is this in any way connected to our individual enhanced performance on either a minor or major scale?

"A richly multicolored mosaic in the reds and greens of a tropical forest, the floor of Broadway's Schubert Theater glowed in the stage lights. Soon the set was ablaze in action, color, and hot Caribbean rhythms. This day and age is so full of wonder: Seattle to New York, downtown, into and out of your hotel, Times Square, the theater, and finally transported into the vivid world of imagination, all in a few hours. We are so able to color our world with the fruits of joy, laughter, and soul.

"The tournament round itself was nondescript, just another business scramble in which my teammates and I played well enough to tie for first place. However, the tournament, sponsored by Seattle Seko Airfreight, was extraordinary: nicely organized, nice golf course, great dinner, great prizes.

"The tie produced a putting contest among the 'A' players. Several ten- to twenty-foot putts were laid out on a practice green, surrounded by fellow contestants and directly under a large balcony deck filled with 'spectators.' Round one eliminated one of three. The unlucky fellow was unable to keep up with the unfolding drama of unconscious, out-of-the-ordinary putting that had ensued. The other two were making every putt.

"Round two comprised the best of five long and twisting efforts. As I recall, it was originally set for three. It's just that three didn't work. Putt number one was barely missed by both of us. Putt number two, left breaking twenty-four feet, was made by both. The crowd, having already watched these guys make three out of three in the prelim, is solid into this. Putt number three, right breaking, maybe twenty feet, was made by both. This is 'getting' interesting. This was supposed to be the last putt. 'Attention, here and now, boys, here and now.' Putt number four was a double breaker, at least thirty feet. I'm first to putt at this point, and something has become really apparent to me by now. I can 'see' every detail, the break, the distance, the feel. No—more accurately, I can 'feel' every detail. My putt tracks the hole precisely, and so does my fellow competitor's. This is now 'getting' to be too much, electric, and cutting into dinner. Putt number five was straight, just fifteen feet. My opponent misses, by nine to ten inches, and I get to watch the improbable once again. My putt is not too soft, not too hard, and not offline! It was a very nice win for me and my teammates, with very pleasant accolades enjoyed during the presentation.

"But I had entered the zone, and it is something to behold. To say that words don't suffice is just not quite good enough, although somewhat accurate. We all have those indescribably 'neat' experiences, don't we? However, somehow, I was connected to those putts. I entered a sphere of almost complete silence, in spite of the clamor resulting from our remarkable strokes. I sort of knew what was happening, and yet I was also distinctively separate from almost all of it, *except* the results. Each putt was a world unto itself, and each putt was going in. . . .

"And I stayed in the zone. I think the whole purpose of this description is not necessarily to report the putting experience that triggered my recognition of the zone but rather to relate more completely the 'aftershocks.' You see, an hour later, I won the raffle: first-class tickets for two on Northwest Airlines to New York City. A few months later, Carol and I were on our way to NYC during the middle of the Gulf War and, in spite of my reservations about traveling then, had a wonderful time. Arriving at our Times Square hotel at 7 P.M. on a Friday evening, we checked in and walked out shortly thereafter into the cold January evening and had a hot time in the old town that night."

Mihaly Csikszentmihalyi, professor and former chairman of the Department of Psychology at the University of Chicago, is the author of a book called *Flow: The Psychology of Optimal Experience*. His work is an exquisite description of many particular aspects of efficient and fulfilling human functioning. The book fulfills its promise, to discuss the psychology of these extraordinary states, and it does so in great detail. It would be a valuable addition to the course of study of any serious "zone" student. Csikszentmihalyi describes eight distinct dimensions of experience reported by people who describe what they feel when they are thoroughly enjoying themselves.

Interestingly, one of these dimensions is that the experience becomes *autotelic,* or worth doing for its own sake. And the significance of this perception is that Zen masters have been saying the same thing for centuries. Zen masters say that the mark of a master is being able to give *full attention* to the activity at hand—no matter how seemingly trivial to others—and doing it to the best of one's ability, *and enjoying it.* This total immersion *in the present,* as you shall learn, is one of the steps on the pathway to the zone. "Staying in the present," of course, has become one of the catch phrases of the sports psychologists, but few offer any effective practical instructions on how to do so. One of the main purposes of this book will be to give you specific methods for mastering this all-important aspect of the the zone.

The autotelic aspect of an activity is commonly reported by athletes during intense competition. For instance, golf professionals often report that they were "not aware of the score," or were "not aware of how they stood in relation to their opponents" until the round was over. It's because their full attention is on the task of the moment, or, to put it another way, they are doing what they are doing for its own sake, with no past or future connotations or considerations.

People who run through their days and constantly think of what they must do next rarely do any one thing to "quality completion." They end the day with a list of "to do's" fully checked off but exhausted from the frantic pace and anxiety. What they don't factor in are the "incompletions" that come back later in the form of emergencies. And it's an endless loop of "catching up." People who operate "in the zone" may only get one task done, but they do it completely and they do it well. *And* they end the day with an energized feeling of fulfillment and exhilaration. Sometimes this way of functioning perpetuates itself, as one efficiently completed act leads to another. When insulated (by intent) from disruptive influence, the zone can become the norm.

In Michael Murphy's classic *Golf in the Kingdom,* Shivas Irons placed as much importance on something as trivial as teeing up the ball as he did on the upcoming shot, or even the results. In fact, he would turn seemingly minor preliminaries into great enhancement exercises. He was tapping into and expanding the holographic principle of interconnectedness with a sort of "karma of physics" where one action results in counteractions. He transformed the simple act of teeing up the ball into a balancing exercise, which in turn carried into and enhanced his swing.

Some of the implications of the principle of interconnectedness will be discussed as we explore the pathways to the zone.

The Common Denominators

Zone experiences tend to have similar characteristics, or common denominators, surrounding them. This has been established through many years of study and research of accounts and descriptions of these events. Included among the many similarities are feelings of lightness, one-pointed attention, being totally in the present, and a definite air of "nothingness" with regard to specific thoughts or technique. It's as if some sort of automatic pilot is activated and set at high levels of efficiency.

Many athletes, when questioned after peak performance, report that they were "not thinking of anything in particular." And that means no negative *or* positive thoughts. Could it be that "being nervous" about an upcoming performance is not so much due to the *apprehension* about the performance but to the *specific steps*—the progression of thoughts and actions—leading up to the performance? In other words, the *importance* builds as the *running thoughts* and *habitual physical rituals* accumulate. And as the importance builds, so does the pressure.

One valuable technique for cultivating zone occurrence is to take inventory of circumstances surrounding these events. To do this, simply record, after every peak performance (or *"zone event"*), as many details as possible—no matter how trivial they may seem—of the circumstances that were present during, just prior to, and just after each event. Over time, you will accumulate an "inventory" of these circumstances—a list—that you can search for common denominators. In this way, you can then *re-create* many if not all of the circumstances that seem to be present when these events occur. You can literally "set the stage" for zone occurrence by ensuring the presence of as many common denominators as possible.

We've all heard of the various "superstitions" subscribed to by top athletes and performers—the "lucky" red shirt, the "lucky" tie, the "lucky" coins—and we've probably all engaged in these types of superstitions at one time or another. What we're really doing is trying to replicate past successes by "setting up" similar circumstances in the form of these superstitions. By finding these superficial common denominators—these "familiar old friends"—that were present during successful performances, we can find comfort levels and increase our confidence. And if we can discover, over time and through careful attention to detail, *several* of these common denominators and then incorporate them into our circumstances as we prepare to perform, we can literally "stack the deck" in our favor.

And there is another way to take advantage of the details surrounding our performances. We can take note, after *poor* performances, of the common denominators appearing at such events and then strive to eliminate them from the circumstances surrounding future attempts. By considering the overview of an event, we can de-isolate the event, treat the entire scenario as an event in itself, dissect the parts, and label them positive or negative.

Over time, you can build an entire storehouse of defining characteristics that have great influence over the outcome of a particular event. Just bear in mind that not one, not two, but many small parts contribute to the whole of a performance. Don't put too much stock in the "lucky" red shirt alone.

Influencing the Determining Factors of Human Performance

Have you ever really wondered why you have "good days" or "bad days"—what the determining factors are? Or have you always simply attributed these to "pure chance"? And what do you think your limits are? Could you run faster than you do now? Could you type faster? Let's take a deeper look at these questions and see how the answers relate to the development of a plan for enhancing *your* performance—in *anything* you do.

First, you must realize that the "type of day" you have is strictly up to you. *How you relate to things* is under your control. "Bad days" happen when you give adversity free rein, and setbacks begin to cluster, or "string out."

There is a wonderful technique for stopping *any* kind of negative momentum dead in its tracks. It's called "The Pause Button," and here's how it works. When something is going wrong—when you get off to a bad start—the first priority should be to momentarily *stop all activity,* hit the "pause button," and break the momentum. Then, to establish a new trend, to set a new course, you must immediately perform something that you know you can do well. In this way you can begin to gather a measure of *positive* momentum, with the chance for a new beginning, one that starts off on the right foot. It really doesn't matter what you do during this pause, even if it is totally unrelated to the activity that you are performing, as long as it is something that you can do very well. An example might be flipping a coin up in the air and catching it a few times, or snapping your fingers, or "drumming" your fingers on something—anything simple and quick that you can perform with ease and confidence.

This is the very same theory that coaches of sports teams apply when they call for a timeout. It's a chance to regroup and stop the downward spiral. But the great coaches don't just *stop* the momentum against their team, they *reverse* it. And the individual, when it comes to momentum, is no different from a team. Performance is partly a product of positive or negative momentum, and the *beginning* moments are critical to establishing a trend.

So *momentum* is very definitely a determining factor of human performance, and it can be gathered or lost during any human activity. But fortunately, it can also be influenced. Most poor performances are the result of "giving up" or just riding out the rest of the performance, resigned to the perception that you just don't "have it" that day. In such cases, negative momentum prevails and the trend is allowed to continue unabated.

It is important to remember that it is never too late to reverse the trend of negative momentum. Every moment can be a new beginning. And if you *always* try to reverse the trend of a poor performance, you minimize the chances of experiencing a string of those kinds of performances, and you can avoid prolonged slumps. Slumps occur when you allow negative momentum to continue unopposed, until finally the flaws overcome all attempts at correct technique. In extreme cases, after very lengthy slumps, the flaws themselves can *become* the technique.

The classic example of this is the person who decides to take up the game of golf but tries to self-teach. Without proper technique from the very beginning, it doesn't take long for bad habits to set in, and to actually *become* that person's technique. It is then very difficult, almost impossible, to change the basic tendencies of that person's technique.

This brings us to the next determining factor of performance, the *beginning*. Whether you're playing chess, tennis, or golf, running a race, studying a textbook—literally anything that you're doing—the way that you *start* is critical. The start of an activity can be influenced in several ways. First on the list, of course, is *adequate preparation,* of which there are two distinct parts, *physical preparation* and *mental preparation*. In a sense, preparation is an integral part of any beginning, as proper preparation should lead into, and blend in with, the activity at hand.

An example of this in physical preparation would be that part of the preshot routine for a golf swing should include *correct practice swings*—and in fact the very best professionals in the world employ just such a technique. I like to call practice swings "preview" swings, because they should preview what you intend to do with the "real" swing, when the ball is present. The same golfer, to prepare "mentally," or psychologically, might "play" the first hole in his mind, in detail, thus getting into a "playing mode" mindset before he even begins the round, thereby avoiding a shaky start.

So *practicing the beginning,* or *preparing for the beginning,* can get you off on the "right foot," and many times that initial momentum will carry on throughout the performance. You might also say that there is a spiritual preparation, but this is on a much broader scale and pertains more to the whole person and his general way of life. But that's not to say that a sincere prayer on the first tee won't help. You never know, and in golf, you need all the help you can get!

Getting *organized* for the beginning is another form of preparation that can influence one's performance in positive ways. Wasn't it Abe Lincoln who said that if he had six hours to chop down a large tree, he'd spend the first four sharpening the blade? Make sure that you are organized before you start your activity or performance. That way you can dedicate 100 percent of your attention to the performance itself, without worrying about distracting incidentals that should have been handled before you started.

The whole concept of the "bad day" is an interesting one. Bad days only happen when you don't stop them *early.* Most people don't say that they're having a bad day until something goes wrong. And interestingly, once something *does* go wrong, and they proclaim that they're having a "bad day," then it's almost as if they must confirm that proclamation by having more things go wrong. In other words, they self-perpetuate their misery. They expect, almost invite, failure. They look for roadblocks to the day instead of taking another road. They feel compelled to validate their own declaration, a declaration *prematurely* decided upon.

The very next time that you hear yourself announcing that you're having a bad day, try this: first, hit the *pause button,* enter the present, get centered, pick up the phone, and call a friend or relative to whom you haven't spoken in quite a while. Spend a few minutes in happy conversation. When you hang up, find something positive to do. Anything at all will do, as long as it is something that you like to do and can do well. When you've finished this, then go on about your day. You have just multiplied your chances for a successful "rest of the day," broken the negative momentum, and stopped a potential "bad day" dead in its tracks.

Remember, there is really no such thing as a predetermined bad day. There are only *bad starts*. And often, the start is the part that we can most positively influence through preparation.

Poor preparation is the harbinger of failure. And most importantly, please remember you can stop whatever you're doing right now, if it's not going well, and *prepare for a new beginning*.

The Zone as a Dynamic or Moving Meditation

It has been said by many masters that *moving meditation*, or meditation in the midst of action, is the most difficult meditation to achieve. Trying to move and act while simultaneously achieving clear and present awareness, single-minded focus— and complete calmness of mind—is indeed a challenge. It is not surprising that when it does occur, it is viewed as a random happening.

As you may have guessed, *moving meditation* and *the zone* are one and the same. And thinking of it in this other way removes a great deal of mystery from the concept and makes its realization more likely the result of intention. This is because the idea of meditation, while remaining esoteric for some, is still regarded as "achievable" with effort.

Meditation is a practice whose quality improves with repeated effort. And we can enter into that state of functioning we call "the zone" more frequently and more effectively if we take the necessary steps and turn them into a *practice*.

To tap the secret of the zone, we must take a more open view of the practice of meditation and study its principles. Those same principles will be the stepping stones that we must follow in order to reach, intentionally and on demand, that state of pure and focused awareness.

Meditation, and particularly "meditation in action," does not mean *not paying attention* to the world going on around you. It means paying attention to *everything* going on around you, at every moment. And it means paying *full* attention to what your attention is on, at that moment. For as far as your mind is concerned, *each moment* is the entire universal consciousness, past and present, timeless and frozen by your full attention.

The true meaning of forever can only be found in the moment.

Constructing the Formulas

In constructing formulas for getting into the zone, we must first form an outline of its elements and accompanying features, and then, working backwards, determine methods for eliciting and then strengthening those elements. Here, then, is the outline of the elements of the zone, with the features of those elements. We will then "fill out" the outline—add meat to the skeleton—with techniques and methods for you to follow and make a practice of, so that you can tailor the routine to your needs. In this way you will maximize the efficiency of your efforts and streamline your path. And farther on, we'll distill the formulas down into a simple, fast, password entry to the zone, regardless of your activity. You'll be able to "switch" into that mode at will, anytime and anyplace.

Elements of the Zone

The state of being in the zone seems to involve certain elements or states of being. In case studies of zone experiences, there are similar reports of experience that seem to be universal, much like the accounts of near-death experiences (NDEs). These are the elements of the zone:

1. Physical well-being (vital and healthy)
   a. feelings of energy
   b. steadiness of nerves
   c. a feeling of being extraordinarily centered
   d. a feeling of lightness

2. Mental well-being and acuity
   a. mental alertness through heightened sensory awareness
   b. rapid and accurate recall
   c. increased creative ability

3. Clear and present focus (special concentration)
   a. an ability to be totally in the present
   b. brain balancing
   c. specific brainwave patterns

These three elements of the zone, and their accompanying features, will be the subject of our thorough investigation. But much more than that, they will lie at the heart of an exciting new possibility for human performance, the possibility that entering the zone can be much more than a random visit by a special grace—that it can be a product of specific action and intention.

Physical Well-Being

The first element is a feeling of physical well-being—feeling very vital and healthy—and is evidenced by *feelings of energy, steadiness of nerves, a feeling of being extraordinarily centered, and a feeling of "lightness"* or being "light on one's feet."

It should come as no surprise that two essential conditions for sustained peak performance in any human physical activity are health and vitality. One common denominator in all sports is exercise and conditioning. If health and physical condition are subpar, then performance is likely to also be substandard.

While zone experiences can occur without the presence of optimum fitness, consistent reoccurrence—and certainly intentional peak performance—is impossible without a measure of physical fitness and good health. And there is a very clear reason for this; it's called *energy*. Feelings of energy, or being "energetic," typify zone experiences. In fact, many athletes, when operating at high levels of performance, describe the experiences themselves as energizing, even though they are seemingly physically exhausted. It's a fact that a sedentary lifestyle results in low energy levels, while a daily regimen of at least moderate exercise can boost one's endurance, overall energy, and health.

Another common denominator in athletic training is a *specialized diet*. While suggested diets differ for various sports and activities, they all contain features that contribute to optimum levels of energy, strength, speed, and endurance. Certain sports (like golf or billiards) and many specialized activities (like intricate surgical techniques) require steady nerves and total control of motor function. In this regard, proper conditioning and a balanced, healthy diet can have great positive influence. Conversely, a non-exercising smoker who pays little attention to a healthy diet would probably exhibit poor motor-skill control and would more than likely show a tendency toward "jumpiness," or nervousness—definite detriments to most activities involving motor skills.

More important than a specific exercise regimen is consistency. While professional fitness trainers can certainly tailor programs to fit the individual and the activities being trained for, consistent exercise is really the key to fitness. Simply walking three twelve- to fifteen-minute miles a day, every day, is one of the healthiest things a person can do. Such exercise keeps the weight down, keeps the heart healthy, promotes good circulation, and keeps the mind sharp. All of this contributes to a "balance of the being," which brings us to the topic of *centeredness*.

Being extraordinarily centered is a feature reported by most people operating in the zone. This not only relates to physical balance but balance of the mind and spirit as well. Having a calm, solid center to return to in times of turmoil is vital to "staying in the game," replenishing one's resources, and contrasts sharply to becoming frantic or desperate and prematurely "spent."

Achieving a physical center involves finding optimum balance. And balance can actually be practiced. Physical balance involves focusing on the body's center of gravity, or "one point." This is located about two finger-widths below the navel. By placing one's mental focus on this spot, attention is drawn away from the head and chest, and there is a de-emphasis of upper-body influence on the balance of the body.

"One-point" awareness, with its balance-enhancing effects, is one of the first things taught to martial-arts students. Many martial-arts disciplines are built around the fundamental of balance. In fact, if you closely examine the movements of any physical human activity, you'll find that efficient performance relies heavily on good balance. Later we will be discussing a balance-enhancing exercise, and finding one's mental and spiritual "one point" or center through the practice of various forms of meditation.

Another common description of the zone experience is that of feeling "light on one's feet." Great running backs seem to skip or float across the football field, and tennis stars exhibit the same extraordinary agility. Muhammad Ali said that he "floated like a butterfly" around the ring, and anyone lucky enough to see him box in his prime would agree that indeed he seemed to do so. Dancers and basketball players seem to defy gravity as they almost levitate during creative and inspired moves. And if you watch little children joyfully at play, the lightness in their step is evident. We will have more on that later.

Of course, exercise and proper diet play a role in promoting this "lightness," but there's more to it. Dancing (and especially wild dancing) is one way to practice lightness and agility and is also thought to release certain chemicals into the bloodstream that encourage "lifting of the spirit." A psychiatrist character in

Golf in the Kingdom said that we could "empty entire wings of mental hospitals with exercise and wild dancing." Inspiration (like music, poetry, or inspirational literature) and sudden insight or unexpected "good news" can bring a "spring to the step," as can seeing a loved one after a long separation. So *joy* seems to be a catalyst for this feeling of lightness, and joy can be found all around us, if we know where to look. We can find it in nature, we can find it in others, and most importantly, we can find it in ourselves. There was a song in the 1960s whose title proclaimed this. It was called "The Wonder of You."

Mental Well-Being and Acuity

These physical states lead to the second recognizable element of the zone and seem to be necessary building blocks toward its occurrence or, more importantly, its intentional construction. This second element is a state of mental well-being and acuity, and its features are *mental alertness through heightened sensory awareness, rapid and accurate recall, and increased creative ability.* And along with this there is a feeling of expectation—prayer energy.

A man who can turn inward is never at the mercy of outer turmoil. This is why it is important to develop a meditation practice—so that you always have a solid, calm center to return to, a "special room" in which to seek safe harbor from life's sometimes turbulent waters. In this center you can find joy and peace, and develop compassion that can be put into practice. It has been said that a foolish selfish man thinks only of himself, while a wise selfish man thinks only of others. The *karma,* you see, comes back to *him.*

All mental activity is better organized and managed when this "special room" exists, and then, paradoxically, physical activity winds up being enhanced. The mind's activity has a direct effect on the performance of the body. The beginningless and endless continuum of consciousness plays out its karmic effects on samsara's physical manifestations. So these thoughts lead us to the realm of mental well-being and acuity, and we will explore the interplay between this realm and the physical activity of the body.

It is important to keep in mind that while mind can influence body—and body influence mind—it is the knowledge and implementation of mental techniques that can "get the ball rolling" in the right direction and, perhaps even more valuable to us, *reverse* the trend of inefficient performance.

Mental alertness is characteristic of peak performance. Correct "on-the-spot" decisions are made, awareness is enlarged or magnified, and sensory cues are much more sensitive and accurate. The opposite of this state would be that of confusion, indecision, and slow or "muddled" thinking.

The state of alertness has a lot to do with not only fitness and quality rest but also draws on sensory perception for clear cues. Strengthening the senses, therefore, strengthens our mental acuity as well. How do we strengthen the senses? One way, of course, is by keeping the sensory receptors clean and healthy, free from disease and contamination. For instance, eye disease or debris in the eye could inhibit sight function, thereby feeding distorted information to the brain.

Another way to strengthen the senses is by practicing *incremental sense enhancement.* This little-known technique has been a practice of esoteric groups (such as ninjas) for centuries, but it has direct practical applications for enhancing human performance.

Here's how incremental sense enhancement works. Let's use hearing for this example. A person can greatly increase the range of his or her hearing by gradually and incrementally expanding it. First, concentration is placed on all sounds within perhaps a 30-foot area. Several times a day, the person actually practices hearing *all* sounds within that relatively small area, regardless of how faint or trivial they may seem. Three twenty-minute sessions a day should be sufficient for most people to learn to *lock in* to every sound in that space. It turns out to be very surprising how many unexpected sounds can be heard after practicing this for a time. Then, after a couple of weeks, the area is expanded to perhaps 100 feet, and the same routine is followed. The area is then gradually expanded, and with each expansion and subsequent period of practice, the "hearing muscles" are gradually strengthened. There are documented studies of people hearing ordinary conversation from distances of 300 yards—the scientifically agreed upon "limit" of human auditory capability.

The same can be done with human sight. Michael Murphy, cofounder of the Esalen Institute and author of several books, including the definitive study on human potential, *The Future of the Body*, has documented reports of golfers seeing coin ball markers on greens 400 yards away!

This strengthening of the senses can have profound effects on performance capability. Judgment abilities are raised, resulting in faster and more accurate decision making. And as sensory-perception abilities are raised, fewer nonessential stimuli get filtered in to contribute to our sensory data. This purifies the cognitive process, resulting in fewer "running thoughts" of random nature. All of this is typical of reported zone experiences.

Another sign of mental alertness is having *rapid and accurate recall ability*. Someone immersed in activity, particularly when in a "pressurized" situation such as an important athletic event or match, typically can recall every specific moment in the event, down to the smallest detail. This is a result of a sort of "purity of thought" that comes with clear and present focus. At the time of the particular "shots" or actions, the participant may be unaware of any thoughts whatsoever but upon completion of the event exhibits total recall.

The ability to recall previous similar actions can be a very valuable asset. Past occurrences can help shape decisions, especially when conditions are similar. As you can see, this is yet another good reason to "set up" similar conditions, such as wearing a red shirt to perform a particular activity that was successful in the past while wearing a red shirt. This is what is meant by working backwards in the chain reaction to produce results at the beginning of the chain reaction. You can refer to my book *Holographic Golf* to see how this works in a practical sense, with the golf swing.

Finally, the ability to instantly innovate in the midst of action, so smoothly that no one is aware—sometimes not even the practitioner—is characteristic of the very best in every field. This remarkable spontaneous *creative ability* is not an accident. It is the result of practice—*the practice of flexibility*, of staying open to "other possibilities." Rigid thinking results in narrow focus, and narrow focus greatly reduces available options. Creativity hits the wall when options cease.

Clear and Present Focus

The third element of the zone experience is clear and present focus, or "special concentration," and it is marked by *an ability to be totally in the present, brain balancing, and specific brainwave patterns.* This third element seems to result from achievement of the first two elements and is part of a definite progression.

An ability to be totally in the present is at the top of the list of "advice" of every sports psychologist, myself included. It is to be *completely absorbed in the moment.* It's one of those things that is easy to say but hard to do. And that's because you can't "try" to do it. It does not work. But you can set the stage for it, and you can cultivate its seemingly random occurrence. When in the zone, you are totally in the present. One of the pathways that lead to this way of being involves *consistency of routine,* which we will discuss later in detail. Absence of routine leads to mental mayhem and running, scattered thoughts, and those will most assuredly lead to turbulent performance—with unpredictable ups and downs.

Brain balancing involves the stimulation of both hemispheres, left and right. Information should be processed by *both* hemispheres in order to get efficient action. So technical details and logic must be used *along with* intuition and creativity.

Finally, much work has been done with brainwave patterns. The EEG Mind Mirror measures brainwave patterns *during* performance, and some extremely interesting discoveries have been made. Athletes, martial-arts practitioners, artists, musicians, poets, and high-level achievers from many practices and human activities have been monitored during peak performance as well as during times of struggle. Incredibly consistent patterns emerge. During high states of achievement—zone experiences—the same brainwave pattern emerges. Anna Wise, protégée of C. Maxwell Cade, inventor of the EEG Mind Mirror, calls it "the *awakened mind* brainwave pattern." We will discuss these fascinating and valuable discoveries in depth, and show you how selective brainwave patterning (intentional configuring of beta, alpha, theta, and delta brainwaves) can help light the way to the zone.

We've now familiarized you with the elements of the zone— the cornerstones. Armed with this knowledge, you will be able to more fully appreciate descriptions of zone experiences reported by top performers from every sport, discipline, and practice as well as "white moments" achieved by average everyday people and weekend warriors.

Knowing Why You're Not in the Zone

A major part of knowing how to access the zone is knowing why you're not presently in it. By identifying where you are in a particular situation or activity, you can pick the appropriate "switch," strengthen the specific area of present involvement, and move immediately into a mode conducive to peak performance of that particular activity.

Let me give you a real-life, practical example of this process in action. In November of 1997, I was in the final round of the Regional PGA Senior Tour Qualifying Tournament in San Antonio, Texas. We had seventy-eight players competing for just twelve spots to advance to the finals in Florida. If you fail to advance from the regionals, you have to wait a whole year to try again, so the pressure of those four rounds is enormous.

I had shot 72-76-69 the first three rounds and *had* to shoot par 72 the last day to qualify. When you *have* to shoot par on a very difficult golf course, against tough competition, on a cold and windy day, the pressure can be stifling. Standing on the fifteenth tee, I was even par for the day, fighting to hold on. Fifteen at Fair Oaks Ranch is the hardest hole on the course—450 yards, par four, into the wind, a very narrow fairway, big trouble on both sides, water right in front of the green that stretches all the way across the fairway, and a small, hard green that you're firing at with a middle to long iron, *if* you smash a *perfect* drive. There is absolutely no room for error.

As we waited (fortunately for me) for the group ahead to clear, I quickly put my "zone training" to work. First, I took a few deep, slow breaths, to cleanse and energize the brain. Then I assessed my needs. I needed to *calm down,* I needed to *energize,* and I needed to focus on my *present goal*—not the goal of qualifying, or shooting 72, but getting *this* drive into the fairway, with really good distance.

To calm down, I immediately did some *"one-point" focusing,* which results in instant centering and balancing. For instant energy, I turned to the trees around the teeing area. I quickly found a large tree that had grown beautiful and graceful throughout many years. I thought of how many years that tree had been there and tried to siphon off some of its awesome energy. I sensed its connection to the earth and how stable it was. And looking at its branches and leaves, I thought of how much life it supported and the shelter it provided. So I literally *drew energy* from that tree, from nature.

Now feeling centered and energized, I shifted my attention to *focusing on my present goal,* that of playing an exceptional tee shot. First, I *visually* found a target area, *pictured* a drive flying down the fairway to that area, and *thought* of how many thousands of times I've produced that very shot on the practice tee. Then I said to myself, "Just hit that drive one more time."

By using *involvement in the moment* (complete attention to the present goal), *positive visualization,* and *positive expectations,* I left no room for negative thoughts to enter and was able to take advantage of my calm, energized state. And then I lined up and swung. The entire process took less than sixty seconds, and most zoning techniques take even less time, sometimes only a few seconds.

The drive that I played there on fifteen was possibly the best of the week, long and dead straight. It ended up about 270 yards down the fairway, in the *geometrical center.* It was perfect. If I'd had to hit that drive twenty years ago, before I knew about these techniques, there's no telling where it would have ended up. The best part of it was that the confidence that I gained after that drive carried me through the rest of the round. I parred fifteen and sixteen, birdied seventeen, and parred eighteen, for a 71 that enabled me to finish in fifth place alone, easily qualifying for the finals.

CHAPTER 2

Techniques for the Ten Pathways to the Zone

We have identified ten pathways that, when followed through repeated practice, lead to states of exceptional human performance. We will now discuss these specific pathways and the various techniques that access them. If you take the appropriate steps, the result will be that you develop the characteristics of the zone state and achieve a level of performance far beyond your "normal" experience. Many times it will only be necessary to implement a single technique for immediate zone entry, and on other occasions you may need to employ several of them. Later, we will show you how best to identify the needed techniques so that you can streamline and expedite zone access.

One reason most people often perform below their potential is that they really don't know what to do to raise their level of efficiency. They waste time and energy with negative self-talk and over-analysis of the mechanics of their activity. They ignore energy, sensory abilities, instinct, and their natural inner force, or *chi*. Here are the ten pathways to the zone with the *techniques* for achieving them.

1. *Creating an energetic feeling.* When energy is needed, keep in mind that mental energy can boost physical energy. The example would be the long-distance runner who gets fatigued but through mental toughness and mental technique breaks through to the "second wind" phenomenon. The runner's mental ability results in a definite "uplifting" of the levels of available physical energy and a prolonging of athletic stamina. Many

times it seems that a person is "exhausted," when in fact that person has given up in his mind, has given in to the challenge—not buying in to the reality that the "game" is not yet over.

How many times has a phone call or letter made you suddenly happy and made you want to "go out dancing"? The surge of energy that you feel is a result of the "happy chemicals" released in your body by the good news. And prior to receiving the unexpected good news you were tired and irritable—and unhappy. It is also true, however, that physical exhaustion can occur as a result of inadequate rest, improper nourishment, physical injury, or lack of exercise. But by far the most common reasons for "tiredness" are stress and unhappiness.

It's a big world that we live in. Nature is vast. And the energy of the universe is at your disposal. You can tap into it anytime you like, but you've got to look for it. *You've got to be able to recognize potential sources of energy and avoid sources of negative energy.* An example of negative energy would be everyone telling you that you *can't* do something or telling yourself that you can't. On the other hand, we've all witnessed the effects of a huge partisan crowd yelling for the home team. Its *positive energy* is inspirational and results in a surge of "extra energy," in individuals and in entire teams.

The *Fifth Insight* of the Celestine Prophecy is an exquisite and complete description of *universal energy* and the ways in which we can tap into it, through nature, others, and, most importantly, ourselves. By breaking free of the chains of *ego,* we can see a clear and unobstructed path to all of the forms of this energy. And far from stealing, robbing, or plundering this energy, we must learn how to share in it in harmony. Since *everything* is ultimately energy in different forms, we must first recognize this, see it in that way, and then find a way to blend with it, and with every *thing* and everybody. In this way we can boost the universal energy, and therefore boost our own. Conflict over energy is only depleting and destructive.

There is a technique by which we can turn any interaction

into a mutual energy-raising exercise—one of those win-win situations for the psyche. The technique is called *transmuting energy*. The way it works is that *anything* of a negative nature that comes into our personal "field," or environment, is immediately moved up to the fourth chakra level, the heart chakra, and then sent back out to its source. Instead of engaging in energy-draining conflict, "both poles" are charged positively, conflict is avoided, and both parties are raised up a level in energy.

Let me give you a real-life example of this in action, an example that I was personally involved in. I was on a trip to Sedona, Arizona, with friends, Judy Bailey and Betsy Biggers. After camping out in Sedona for a few days, and then hiking the Grand Canyon, we headed back to Phoenix. Judy and Betsy (a psychotherapist) are both very evolved and conscious people and very assertive with each other. This mix always provides some "stimulating" conversation—and amusement for me.

Judy has this little habit where she likes to finish your sentence for you, cutting you off in the process. She's the type who will let you tell a joke and then blurt out the punch line for you. This irritates Betsy to no end, and she constantly reminds Judy of her dislike for this habit. Well, it happened one time too many as we were driving, and once again Betsy began telling Judy of her frustration and how she had repeatedly asked her not to do this. Of course, a heated discussion ensued, more heated than usual.

When we stopped to eat lunch, I got Betsy aside and taught her how to *transmute energy*. After explaining the concept to her, I told her that the next time Judy finished a sentence for her, to say to Judy, with absolutely no sarcasm and with total sincerity, "You know, I've really reflected on my anger about this in the past, and I've come to see that it really is a compliment to me that you are *so tuned in* to me, that you *listen* to what I have to say with *such interest,* that you're able to finish my sentences for me. I really feel good about that, because so many people don't really listen very well."

About fifteen minutes into the continuation of the drive, Betsy got her chance, and it worked like a charm. It was obvious that Betsy had thought about it and had bought into the concept *with sincerity*. It worked like a charm, and it was fascinating to watch this process at work. By taking in what she had perceived as negative energy and moving it up the chakras to a higher level, she transmuted (changed) her own negative energy about the situation, and in the process gave Judy a little "happy surprise"—a gift of positive energy—and made *her* feel happy as well.

The key to this technique, of course, is sincerity. As the great Indian saint, Neem Karoli Baba (known to his devotees as Maharajii), professed, and this was his anthem, his great legacy—*"Love everyone, and tell the truth."* This means that when you say that you love *everyone,* make sure that you're telling the truth. And it means that if you say that you don't like someone, then you must be missing something. Find what you're missing in him, and then you can tell the truth when you say that you love him.

So even seemingly negative situations in life can be sources of positive energy, if we train ourselves. We must learn, through practice, to constantly ask ourselves the question, "In *this* moment, where is the energy?"

2. *Steadying the nerves.* Typically, when we're "nervous," we either slow down or speed up. About to give a speech in front of a large crowd, the inexperienced public speaker "freezes up," forgets what to say, and practically falls into a confused stupor. The nervous comedian's timing, so essential to effective comedy, is thrown off, resulting in an embarrassing silence or, worse yet, a patronizingly polite smatter of applause. On the other hand, the nervous golfer's swing gets faster and faster, completely out of sync. In all cases, *timing and rhythm* are lost, which leads to all sorts of mechanical breakdown.

There are two main reasons, resulting from fear, for these changes in one's rhythm. First, the breath becomes shallow and quick, a physical response to a mental activity, and second, there is a dramatic increase in the "running thoughts" that so typify nervous confusion. When running thoughts are abundant, we literally "don't know what to do next."

Fortunately, there are several techniques that can restore timing and rhythm very quickly, before the negative momentum gets out of hand and a lengthy "slump" begins. When rhythm and timing are disrupted for long stretches, we run the risk of establishing faulty habits. That's how slumps evolve and linger.

The first thing that a nervous person should do to calm down is the oldest trick in the book: take long, slow, deep breaths for at least two minutes. From my career in competitive golf, I can tell you that it really works like magic—*if you do it right!* If you do it wrong—either too fast, too shallow, or for only thirty seconds or a minute—it won't work at all, and you'd be surprised how many people just won't do it correctly. It took me a long time to realize that it really works if you do it the right way. When the mind and body are racing, a few deep breaths seem to take forever, when only maybe thirty or forty seconds go by. You've got to slow things down, and give it time to work.

One additional benefit of deep, slow breathing is that when done for a long enough time, say two minutes or more, it gives the mind enough "quiet time" so that it, too, can relax and slow down, allowing the running thoughts to subside. The unfocused mind, the one fraught with running thoughts, is the enemy of concentration. It *wastes* the moment. People who have an overabundance of running thoughts are always thinking of what they're going to do next and consequently never pay full attention to the moment. Jackson Browne, the consummate rock poet, said it best in his great song "Your Bright Baby Blues." Browne sings, "No matter where I am, I can't help thinking I'm just a day away from where I want to be."

There are some wonderfully effective techniques for quelling the running thoughts that invade and take over one's consciousness. Later, when we discuss brainwave patterns, we'll be taking a closer look at some of these.

For now, let's concentrate on trying to get more into the moment. As you read this, notice your *quality of attention.* Let the sentence and its full meaning sink in. Speed reading aside, you should absorb each sentence completely and understand it fully before beginning another. Don't ignore words that you are not familiar with. Stop, grab the dictionary, learn the word, and then read the sentence again. You'll get more meaning from it. You'll learn more and consequently enjoy it more. And you'll feel better about yourself, less rushed and less stressed. *Complete* what you're doing, with attention to the smallest detail, and then go on. If you keep skimming over everything in your life, getting it half-done, you're also cutting your fun in half, to say nothing of your self-esteem. If you want to grasp the meaning of *completion* and *accomplishments,* and how it makes you feel, just think back to the moment when you were handed your very first paycheck.

Another way to steady the nerves is to *replay past successes.* If you're not particularly adept at visualization, try to remember the *feeling* of successfully completing an activity. Feel again, in your memory, the joy of finishing that table you made with your own hands, or of completing that painting. Relive that sense of *mastery* you felt when you aced your tennis opponent at match point or blasted a drive thirty yards farther than your playing partners on the golf course.

All of us can draw on past successes and relive the feelings connected to them. This type of *associative recall* can be a powerful ally when similar situations present themselves. A technique like this one replaces fear with a surge of confidence, and it can begin to calm the primary demon of performance— the negative thought.

One more thing about negative thoughts; remember that they can only creep in when the mind is idle or confused. When the mind is filled with positive thoughts or images, or when it is intensely focused on a set routine, there is no room for the negatives to get in. But if they do make their way in, how you handle them can make all the difference. Don't fight a negative thought. Let it come in, and *explore* it. Wait it out, and train yourself to emerge from the exploration with a "home base" positive thought, one that is your *standard next thought* after a negative one. In this way, you will never allow negative thoughts to take root, and you'll never string them out and allow a trend to become established. It's like a golf tip I once received from one of my teachers, the best mental tip I've ever had. My teacher said, "When you hit a bad shot, within seconds after hitting it, start figuring out how you can make your *next* shot a really great one. By doing this, you greatly eliminate the chances of 'stringing out' bad shots—and holes." If you "stew" over the bad shot too long, the negative attitude will breed more bad ones, and the trend will self-perpetuate.

One note to remember if your activity requires steadiness or controlled precision: Any or *too much* caffeine can cause "jumpiness" or unsteadiness of hand. It is better to avoid it prior to an important performance or one in which you must maintain a slow and steady rhythm. Caffeine can cause you to "speed up" from your normal rhythm or pace.

3. *Centering.* Centering and balance—and in many ways they are synonymous—should always be the primary fundamental in learning *any* human activity. A strong and always-available center provides safe harbor from the storms of life, a quiet private place accessible to us at any time, anywhere, and allows us to rejuvenate before venturing out once more. Without a center, we are guaranteed to be tossed about at the total mercy of life's tempests.

Centering is an important early lesson in Eastern traditions and is part of nearly everyone's daily practice in that part of the globe. How the Western world could use such a practice! But more and more people in our culture are becoming aware and mindful of the importance of centering, as practices such as meditation and tai chi become less esoteric. By stilling the body and the mind, we can find that center, that harbor of the soul, and through repeated practice strengthen it and expand it. With time and devotion, *we* can literally become a center of power.

In order to tie together the concepts of centering and balance, let's take a look at the martial arts. The very first thing that many martial-arts students learn, particularly those studying aikido, is the centering technique of "one-point" awareness. You'll recall that the "one point," for everyone, is located at a point about two finger-widths below the navel. This is the body's center of gravity.

Here's how "one-point" awareness is taught: the student is first told to stand on one leg for as long as possible. Typically, the exercise does not last long, as the student begins to waver and loses his balance rather quickly. Then, the student is told to stand on the one leg again, but this time he is told to keep two fingers (index and middle) on his "one point." With *awareness* now focused on the center of gravity, the student can stand, perfectly balanced, for long periods—as long as the mental focus stays on the "one point," or fatigue sets in.

The reason that the student could not last very long on the initial attempt is because without "one-point" awareness, the mental focus, the emphasis, stays up, in the mind (running thoughts) and in the chest and upper body (emotions), and this "top-heaviness" results in a loss of balance. Imagine the effect of this extreme top-heaviness on an athlete, for whom optimum balance is essential.

Now, once the student becomes familiar and comfortable with his "one point," he is taught to stand on one leg *without touching* his center but with his *mental focus* there. With the mind and emotions directed at the center, *it* becomes the target of the emphasis, and perfect balance is achieved.

I have had amazing success and dramatic results using this technique on my golf students at my teaching center, the Holographic Golf Institute. First I teach them "one-point" awareness using the martial-arts methods described above, and then I teach them to address the ball with their mental focus on their center, their "one point," instead of on the ball, club, or their hands. You should see the results. There is dramatic immediate improvement, as they employ centrifugal force, working outward from their center, instead of using the hands to slash *at* the ball. All of a sudden, because of learning how to physically center, the dog wags the tail instead of the other way around.

As you develop awareness of your center and find yourself residing there more and more, you'll come to view it as a safe, quiet, and private place. This center represents not only your *physical* center, or balance point if you will, but it can also become "home base" for your mind.

The strongest meditation is when an empty focus is brought to an empty center. That's when we become pure awareness. Meditation is the practice of centering the mind, and doing balancing exercises using the "one point" is the practice of centering the body. Done together, they solidify and strengthen the mind-body connection, resulting in a remarkably harmonious state of pure awareness that, when achieved in the midst of activity, defines that extraordinary state of functioning called "the zone."

It is important for you, the serious zone student, to cultivate a relationship with your center, with both body and mind. Practice the physical one-leg balancing exercises regularly. This practice also trains you in the art of *placement of mental focus.* These abilities will prove to be strong allies as your zone practice progresses. Also develop a practice of "just sitting," not necessarily Zen sitting, but just sitting still, and placing your mental focus on your center. You'll find that the longer you can keep it there, the more centered you'll become. The ultimate goal, of course, is to be able to go to this center, with both mind and body, in the midst of action. This ability to center at will, to "call up" this *moving meditation,* even when your surroundings are in utter turmoil, will be your psychological "hole card." When you see and feel the results of such practice, it will become your primary objective for all aspects of your life.

Once you become adept at centering and balancing, you can apply the skill to *any* activity that you may be involved in. You can apply it to any sport, and with it you can become a better dancer. You can de-escalate an argument immediately, and you can use it to calm down before giving a speech or a business report to the stockholders in the boardroom. You can use it in parenting, when trying to deal patiently with your teenagers. Musicians, doctors, and dentists can use it, as can patients, or restless employees whose anger is boiling over in the picket line. The applications for centering are endless.

Perhaps one of centering's greatest benefits is that it puts you into a state where other zone-provoking techniques can effectively be used. Centering is not only an end in itself but a preparatory step as well. Introduced into your life as a regular practice, it can become not only a stress reliever but a *stress eliminator.*

No matter what facet of your life you'd like to improve, this centering *practice* will do the trick. But it must be a consistent, ongoing practice, in every sense of the word. The great thing about this practice is that it can be done anywhere, anytime— before, after, or *during* any activity. Just keep reminding yourself, constantly, to put your mental focus in your center. And remember that when you do, you're getting it out of the arena of running thoughts and emotion.

In the world we live in, with its daily atrocities of man against man and man against the environment, we all need a place of retreat and quiet solitude. Some have sailboats or yachts, and some have beach villas or country houses. But you don't need those things if you know that the most private place on earth is right inside of you, waiting to be discovered.

4. *Achieving a light feeling.* Being "light on one's feet" has long been associated with athletic prowess. The athleticism and grace of a world-class dancer or gymnast is marked by this ability to "float" through the air, feet touching the ground only for an instant before launching into yet another stunning series of acrobatic moves. The ice skater, the running back in

football, and the tennis player all rely on agility, quickness, and grace as they slide, shift, and bounce their way around their various arenas. And how about the boxer, whose quickness and ability to "dance" around the ring greatly contributes to victory or defeat? I think of Muhammad Ali in his prime, although weighing well over two hundred pounds, exhibiting the "lightness of foot" of an eighty-five-pound Nadia Comaneci, the consummate Olympic gold medal gymnast. And how about basketball's *Michaelangelo*—who hasn't seen Michael Jordan perform his gravity-defying moves, where he seemed to hang in the air longer than gravity should allow? Any physical action requiring agility and quickness can be performed better when one "feels light" and able to move quickly with little effort.

Throughout religious literature there are accounts of saints, masters, and other "enlightened beings" displaying levitational abilities. *Lightness,* "halos," and auras have always, in many well-known *and* some esoteric traditions, been featured and depicted in religious art.

Some consciousness evolutionists believe that as we evolve our spirituality, we (as pure energy) will vibrate at higher and higher frequencies until we become "lighter than air" and ultimately disappear to the naked human eye. We will still "be there" but in a different energy form. At that point, they say, free from our heavy and cumbersome bodies, we will travel by means of awareness and intent. This "lightness," so often associated with advanced states of functioning, is a trait well worth developing.

In some cultures, notably our own in America, overeating has become a serious problem. While obviously a health risk and detriment, being overweight due to unhealthy eating habits also drastically reduces agility, quickness, energy, and the general quality of the way we feel, physically and emotionally. In addition, pertinent to our current discussion, another negative effect is felt. The possibility for achieving "lightness of foot" is greatly reduced, and a marked drop in athletic ability is experienced. Any physical activity requiring agility, quickness, or stamina—not to mention sufficient energy levels—becomes automatically more difficult to perform, and quality of performance drops significantly.

So diet, then, is an important ingredient in the recipe for peak performance. And proper diet certainly contributes greatly to the "lightness" that we seek to feel.

How else can we promote that feeling? Through specific drills and exercises, we can train ourselves to be "light on our feet" more often, and we can learn to "call up" the feeling anytime, anywhere.

First is the "drift" drill: We're all familiar with the sight of world-class tennis players as they await service. They stand, in a semicrouched position (low center of gravity), and sway left and right, over and over again, as they try to time and *blend* their movements to those of their opponent. By doing this, they stay "light on their feet" and ready to move in any direction. It gives them a "jump" on things. You've probably seen football players at practice doing agility drills where they step in and out of tires that are staggered forward, left and right.

Running in place, using your toes and the balls of your feet, is a great way to practice "being light on your feet." And you'll find that when walking, if you try to "walk from your center," it adds a dimension of "quality" to the walking motion. You should be aware, too, when walking, of having a "spring to the step."

Another way to get that light, bouncy feeling is to *listen to music* that makes you feel that way. We all have favorite types of music that make us feel happy and buoyant, that make us want to move to its rhythm. It's a wonderful way to lift the spirits or make us feel light and energetic.

Whenever you feel down, or "heavy," try this for something different. Go to a playground filled with children, and watch them play for a while. There is nothing more uplifting than to see these "little beings of pure awareness and light" as they skip, bounce, and laugh their way through their fantasy (?)

world. There is this line from the poem "Point the Way to Hell":

> If young forever you could stay,
> We'd spare you from our sins;
> I wonder where the line is crossed
> That weans you from your whims.

This idea of "lightness," so evident on the playground in the faces of the children, can brighten and enhance *anything* you do.

5. *Becoming alert through heightened sensory awareness.* You might say that "being alert" is *being aware of signals from our surroundings.* It is the input to our senses that shapes our perceptions. What we see, hear, feel, smell, or taste in our environmental field dictates our thoughts and actions. It is vitally important, then, that we make full use of our senses in every way possible. In *Holographic Golf,* I say, *"When we make full use of our senses, our minds have more ammunition with which to influence the movements of our muscles."* So the question becomes, how do we make full use of our senses?

First we must pay more attention to them. When we just take them for granted, we miss out on many subtleties that could enrich our experiences. By focusing more intently, for example, on the shape and texture of a tree, we can come to appreciate more what an amazing and beautiful structure it really is. In this way, we strengthen not only our universal bond with nature, but we strengthen our visual perception as well. Zone experiences typically feature a *heightened sensory awareness,* where visual details are more evident, colors are more vivid, and in general the person is more "in tune" with his surroundings.

In the section on the elements of the zone we discussed a technique called *incremental sense enhancement,* a method for strengthening the senses. Sometimes, in certain situations, all that is needed for entry into the realm of peak performance is the springboard of *closer attention to detail.* In golf, for example, poor putting can sometimes be traced to simply not inspecting the contours of the green closely enough. In other words, looking at the green with *more scrutiny,* with more attention to detail, can shed new light on how the ball might roll. Sometimes a basketball player who is missing free throws only needs to focus more intently on the *center* of the net to snap out of the slump. In other words, *see* the target in more detail. The noted sports psychologist Dr. Bob Rotella calls it getting *target specific.* Have you ever listened to music that you enjoy and then listened to it on a really good sound system with high-quality headphones? The difference is amazing, and you can hear notes that you'd never heard before!

Michael Murphy, in his epic work *The Future of the Body,* wrote eloquently of a sense-enhancing technique called *synesthesia,* or the stimulation of one sense by another. Murphy writes, "For some people, this 'crossing of the senses' is highly developed and the source of great enjoyment and creativity." He goes on, "Both Rimski-Korsakov and Scriabin vividly associated E major with *blue,* A flat with *purple,* and D major with *yellow.* Baudelaire wrote a sonnet about correspondences between fragrances, colors, and sounds, and helped inspire the Symbolist movement's celebration of *synesthesia.* "

So for our purposes, using synesthetic exercises (deliberately crossing the senses) can strengthen the senses so that *observation of subtlety* is more easily achieved. The resultant elevation of perception moves us a step closer to those special realms, those levels of peak performance called "the zone."

It is interesting to note that when one sense shuts down, another seems to automatically strengthen, as if to compensate. It seems to be nature's safeguard. Often, blind people have extraordinary auditory or tactile capabilities. Helen Keller, for example, could *feel* colors with unerring accuracy.

In *Beyond Golf* (Stillpoint, 1996), I touched on this topic when I suggested that golfers practice with headphones, listening to some favorite or inspirational music. After a while, your swing picks up the rhythm, and your whole sense of timing is enhanced, producing smooth, rhythmic power. Stimulation of the senses can increase alertness—a feature of, and a step to, the zone.

6. *Displaying rapid and accurate recall abilities.* In the midst of action, whether it be the playing field or the boardroom, the classroom or the company volleyball tournament, we draw on past experience as we improvise, strategize, and carry out a "plan of attack." It has been said that history can be our greatest teacher, *if* we can remember its lessons.

Peak performance is always marked by the ability to come up with stunning innovations, at just the right, critical time, and to the uninitiated these improvisations seem to just "come out of nowhere." But the fact is, from the moment of birth, we are "stocking the shelves" with information about our world, information that we constantly access and then update as we live our lives, moment by moment. For example, ever since experiencing our first severe summer thunderstorm, we take notice of bad weather's impending arrival, with the advance signs of wind, thunder, lightning, and temperature and pressure changes. As the years go by, and we experience more and more of these storms, our sense of the approach of these events grows sharper. Through *accumulated experience,* we become more "tuned in" to subtle changes in our environmental field. You might say that we've *practiced remembering.*

So it is clear, then, that the ability to remember can have profound effects on our present and future actions. One of the common denominators of high achievers is the "steel-trap mind"—quick thinking made possible by rapid and accurate recall. What's happening with these individuals is an efficiently operating system of *remembering similar circumstances,* drawing on the positive aspects of those past experiences, and then applying current conditions to shape the most efficient present action. What appears to be the spontaneously creative work of a brilliant virtuoso is really the display of an efficient performance by an unfettered *remembering machine.*

There are ways to strengthen our recall abilities. For one,

exercising the "memory muscle" is vital to keeping our *mind files* readily available. In the evening, for instance, spend a few minutes going back over the day's events in detail. Remember (replay) not only the general events but as many surrounding specific details as possible, right down to the sounds, smells, and tastes associated with the events. Also, recall the feelings associated with the day's happenings. All of these details will serve to *root* the memory firmly in the mind, and also keep it "fresh," so that future searches for the information won't have to dig very deep in order to access it. Wasting valuable time "trying to remember"—searching the memory banks—is a leading cause of performance failure. Instead of being able to focus totally on the moment, instinctively accessing similar past experience, we remain suspended in action and waste energy while the attention shifts to search mode. And so the moment, and the chance for quick, instinctive action, is lost.

Memory courses are very worthwhile, and some are very effective in improving associative memory. But the real value of the various memory courses and techniques is in the *memory practice.* Like any other skill, practice enhances it.

7. *Showing creativity in the midst of action.* We've all seen the moves, the heart-stopping innovations that are the trademark of athletes like Venus and Serena Williams, Katarina Witt, Tiger Woods, Brett Favre, Kobe Bryant, Shaquille O'Neal, and others. Such abilities are also exhibited by musicians, actors and actresses, great speakers, great comedians, and many other standouts from all walks of life—*breaking into* unplanned maneuvers that leave us open-mouthed with wonder. Michael Murphy calls such improvisations the "sudden glimmer," a right-brain inspiration that seems to come from nowhere. When such abilities are combined with technical skill and mechanical muscle memory grooved by years of practice, the results can be spectacular to watch and awe-inspiring. This special creativity seems to spring from a number of sources.

First, there is a *framework of disciplined routine,* honed by constant and endless repetition. Ben Hogan, the greatest ball striker in the long history of the game of golf, was also the game's most devoted and prolific practicer. His long hours at the practice tees are legendary. And Michael Jordan practiced the fundamentals of the game of basketball every day. Also well documented are the practice habits of Jerry Rice, arguably the greatest wide receiver in the history of professional football.

But within that framework of disciplined routine is an unrestricted freedom for option—the option of *reactive expression.* What this means is that the practitioner (and let me remind you that the term *practitioner* refers to *anyone* performing *any* activity) is, while following the course of his experiential training, at the same time constantly tuned in to his surroundings and staying open to signals that direct him to more efficient pathways. Thus you have the "sudden glimmer," the unexpected detour, and that detour culminates in brilliant innovation, often in the midst of furious action. The spontaneity does not "spring from nowhere." It is dictated *by the circumstances of the moment.*

During the research of interview and observation, it has become obvious that people who access the zone are extremely *aware*—aware of their complete *environmental field* (the surroundings detectable through the senses) and everyone and everything in it, often in minute detail. In criminology, it is called "observation of commonplace" and is a learned (*and* instinctive) skill possessed by top-notch detectives. It involves arriving at a crime scene and observing things in such detail as to see things that others don't. The answers are always there, but the clues must be observed in order for conclusions to be drawn. And as a basketball player streaks down the court, surrounded by three defenders, there always exists an optimum move that will elude them all. A player operating in the zone will find that move, seemingly with instinct, but what is really happening is that his observation of commonplace, coaxed into action through deeply focused sensory awareness, gives him the feedback he needs to find the perfect move.

So how can we practice spontaneous creativity? There are

three primary techniques for encouraging a more versatile arsenal of performance skills: (1) *seeing things in more detail,* (2) *focusing on sensory feedback,* and (3) *practicing imagination.*

First, practice going into a room and seeing the room in as much detail as you can. Notice things you've never noticed before. You'll be surprised at what you see. In time and with frequent practice just a couple of minutes a day, this type of attention will become a habit, and your perception of detail will become much more acute. Others will notice pretty quickly that you seem sharper, more "with it." Just like with any other skill, you simply have to practice to improve.

Next, you'll want to develop your sensory feedback. Anywhere that you are (a great time is when you're *waiting*), you can practice this inherent skill. Simply pay more attention to the sights, sounds, and smells around you. As you practice and strengthen your sensory feedback, you will, for instance, *hear more* in that waiting room, you'll *notice smells* (like perfumes or colognes) more, if you try, and you'll *see* with greater clarity and detail, perhaps the details of what someone is wearing or pictures on the walls. On the golf course, or even in your own backyard, focus on the color and texture of the trees more than you ever have before.

Lastly, you can *practice imagination.* Just do things in different ways, intentionally. Try variations. *Throw a ball* for an hour with your nondominant hand. *Brush your teeth* with the opposite hand. Drive a different route to work and yet another route home. Explore the endless possibilities of the world around you. *Nothing can atrophy the imagination more than boredom, because along with boredom comes sameness, and sameness leaves the other possibilities unexplored and unpracticed.*

With time, you'll see the world around you in a new and more beautiful way. The fast pace of our lives sometimes obscures nature's beauty from our view. But it's always there, and so is the zone. And like the basketball player streaking down the floor, you can, by *looking for it* from within your own collective information, find it every time. By elevating your focus and perception, you can reach that dimension of excellence that lies just beyond the ordinary. *You* can find the optimum move.

In *The Legend of Bagger Vance: A Novel of Golf and the Game of Life,* there is a passage to the effect of: "Have you ever seen an eagle soar, Michael? Or watched a shark glide through the water? Don't you sense observing them that each bank of a wing, each adjustment of a fin, is its most optimum selection from infinite possibilities? Don't they seem . . . guided flawlessly by instinct?"

8. *Staying totally in the present.* It's the mantra of the modern-day sports psychologist (and I am in that number), to "stay in the present." The obvious reason for this universal advice is that you're liable to "botch the moment" if you try to perform while thinking of the past or worrying about the future. And this phenomenon of absorption in the task at hand marks every account of zone experiences.

Many sports psychologists offer various "tricks" and techniques for achieving this mindset, but often what they are really doing is "talking about something" instead of *saying something.* Fortunately, there is a time-tested, centuries-old, proven method for cultivating this important way of thinking. It has long been a "mantra of action" for monks, ascetics, Zen masters, and people of various disciplines everywhere. The method involves performing every single act, no matter how seemingly trivial, with complete attention and focus. And the reality of it is that *nothing—and no act—*is trivial. If you're sweeping out the garage, you do it with complete attention, and you try to do the best job of sweeping that's ever been done in the history of the world. And you do *everything* that you do that way. In this way, every act becomes a *practice* and doing things *that way* becomes a *practice,* and eventually it becomes a way of life. The fact is, if you do something with less than your full attention, it is likely to be done with less proficiency. Quality will be lost.

The trouble is, in many parts of our fast-paced world today, we feel as if we have to rush about with a helter-skelter schedule in order to get everything done. And therein lies the problem—the schedule is overloaded to begin with, and priorities get buried under a mountain of erroneously perceived "must do's." So the first step is to do a better job of *scheduling* our lives, and of prioritizing things. With this first step, we are then free to give our attention fully to each task or activity.

Another way to encourage this ability of staying in the present is by developing a consistent routine, or *way* of doing things. By focusing on how you are going to go about doing something, it leads into it and keeps your mind occupied with the task at hand. For example, when you are getting ready to return service in a tennis match, it is better to focus on and preview your intended actions rather than thinking of where you are going to go to dinner that evening. By *leading into the action* with *pertinent* and *appropriate* thoughts on that action, you are, in a sense, already into the action. But when you are suddenly faced with performing on the spur of the moment, with absolutely no lead-in, no "warm-up," you may get into an unwanted trend right off the bat, as you struggle for the "groove." The struggle may last throughout the action, and hence the poor performance.

In teaching golf I place a great deal of emphasis on the *preshot routine.* I try to teach the student to develop a routine that not only is consistent in detail but also harbors elements that enhance the performance of the swing itself—a set of built in "minidrills." This is a very powerful and much overlooked teaching technique, and the importance of it is exemplified every week on the PGA Tour. Every tour player, without exception, has such a routine.

Scott McCarron, one of the top players on the tour and ranked in the top forty players in the world, told me that replicating his routine is *the only thing* that he thinks about on the course during competition. Scott said that even his habit of tugging on his glove is a carefully orchestrated ritual that must be the same every time. He actually counts the tugs. But this seemingly meaningless detail serves another important purpose other than ensuring consistency. It keeps his mind occupied with something *in the present.*

George Knudson, the late Canadian who was considered perhaps the finest ball striker since Ben Hogan, and the winner of many important tournaments, was an ardent practitioner of the "inner game." Knudson said that he would "count steps" from shot to shot, not for the purpose of calculating yardage, but to simply occupy the *time between shots.* And basically he went on to say that when you "let the mind wander," it will inevitably drift to past occurrences, future possibilities, or negative thoughts of some kind, and the quality of attention to the upcoming shot is either diluted or negatively tainted. It's better to keep the mind occupied with something like a mantra, in order to keep it away from possible negative thought.

So remember that you can *set the stage* for zone experiences by giving your actions your full undivided attention and by not making the mistake of considering any action "trivial." If you think of enough acts as trivial, and tend to them as such, you will groove that mode of operation into a habit, and it will become increasingly more difficult to "shift modes" when faced with some important performance or task.

9. *Balancing the brain.* Peak performers, top athletes, enlightened beings, authentic religious masters, people operating "in the zone," "special" people (world leaders and famous celebrities), charismatic people, and anyone "doing what they do" to the very best of their abilities display clearness, brightness, and balance of the *eyes.* Both sides of the face appear equally balanced. You don't see a "dull look" in either eye, you don't see one eye half-closed, and you don't see more wrinkles on one side than the other. And there is a reason for this: their brains are more *balanced* than that of the ordinary person.

We know that the "left side" of the brain is the cognitive, logical, problem-solving side while the "right side" is the creative, imaginative, intuitive side. From the right side of the brain comes the "sudden glimmer," the inspired, instinctive, spontaneous innovation. And we also know that the "left brain" controls the right side of the body, while the "right brain" controls the left side.

For the brain to be in a "state of balance," both sides must be used or *exercised*. And without an adequate, balanced amount of activity, the underused side will, like any other function or muscle, atrophy. Brain hemisphere atrophy shows clearly on the face. The most comprehensive research on this subject has been done by Martin Sage, founder of the Sage Learning Method. Sage Productions has offices and practitioners all over the world and is silently working its magic, helping groups and individuals to elevate their performances to their highest potential.

The next time you notice someone who has been stuck in a mundane, unchallenging job for a long time, a job that requires no creativity, take a look at his left eye. What you'll see is an eye that is dull, probably partly closed, and devoid of any "light," and more than likely the entire left side of the face will seem sad. What's happening here is that the left eye is showing what is going on with the right side of the brain—*nothing*. There is no "action," no exercise, no *creative play*. But if you go up to that person and start asking him what he really enjoys doing the most, or about his children or loved ones, anything of great interest or meaning to him, you can just see him "light up" right before your eyes. Just that little bit of right-brain stimulation is enough to change his facial structure.

What Sage is doing is stimulating both sides equally so that the result is balance—balance of the two sides of the brain *and* the two sides of the face. When you leave one of Sage's seminars (and I have left several of them), you literally look at least ten years younger, you feel happier and "fuller," and there is a lightness in your step and in your spirit. And he gives you ways to reinforce the balance every day. Sage has a favorite saying: "Whatever it is that you like to do the most, whatever 'lights you up,' *someone* is making a living at it." He explores that with you and helps you to make it a reality. He is *transforming lives*.

So in order to elevate your performance level, reach your potential, and live a happier, more balanced life, you have to make sure that you pay attention to adequately exercising both sides of your brain. Some ways to stimulate the right brain are reading, puzzle solving, creating (writing, building something fun, gardening), or perhaps just exploring—anything that activates your imagination.

Interesting and revealing brain studies are being made all over the world, and it is becoming clear that brain-side usage and function has a lot to do with behavior patterns. What's exciting is that we can, more than we ever thought possible, alter these patterns by controlling the way we use our brain—the ultimate computer.

10. *Creating specific brainwave patterns.* Much work has been done in this area, and from it come some very interesting and applicable techniques that promise to enhance all human performance, as well as quality of life in general. Brainwaves of people who are "in action" are measured by what is called the EEG Mind Mirror, a variation of standard EEG measurement discovered by the late C. Maxwell Cade. The four brainwaves measured are beta, alpha, theta, and delta.

Using the EEG Mind Mirror, Cade and his protégée, Anna Wise, measured the brainwaves of people performing at their highest levels, people in the zone. Athletes, musicians, artists, poets, writers, great chefs, and others, from a variety of fields, were measured while performing their specialty, and performing it extremely well. They were measured when they were in the zone. And from this data, some astounding, irrefutable results were obtained.

Every one of the subjects measured and tested exhibited extremely similar patterns of brainwaves during peak performance. Cade and Wise went on to call this pattern the *awakened mind pattern.* These similar patterns in all of these people featured *low beta, higher alpha,* and similar combinations of the other two, theta and delta.

Beta brainwaves indicate the "busy mind," the *running*

thoughts, and when beta content is high, the mind can be in disarray, overloaded, and, in extreme cases, disoriented. When your mind is in chaos, you have too many running thoughts and your beta brainwaves are at high levels.

On the other hand, peaceful, quiet states, meditative states, and states of pure awareness and clear concentration are typified by higher alpha and lower beta brainwave levels. It seems that people who are consistent peak performers, people who are "tops in their field," tend to exhibit these specific brainwave patterns.

Wise, after the death of her mentor, went on to study and research the findings even further. And as her work evolved, she began to find that certain activities seemed to stimulate specific brainwaves. Her intention became to find ways for ordinary people to enter into these awakened mind patterns at will, by performing techniques that bring about these particular combinations of brainwave patterns.

Let's take a look at a practical example of one of these techniques, one that you can put to personal use *today.* Running thoughts—the disorganized mind—means high beta brainwave measurements. When we have running thoughts or a busy mind, even if we don't speak out loud we *subvocalize.* And when we subvocalize, the *tongue moves.* Now, if we deliberately *"still the tongue,"* just hold it still in the center of the mouth and continue to *consciously hold it still* for at least three minutes, we stop subvocalizing, we reduce running thoughts, and we experience a dramatic reduction in the levels of beta brainwaves. The alpha brainwaves increase, and we begin to enter into the initial stages of a meditative state. We calm down, our right brain engages, and we open up to all sorts of valuable feedback. We become receptive to the "sudden glimmer." We are on the doorstep of the zone.

The implications of this work are astounding as well as transformational. In effect, what this means is that we are *all* peak performers, capable of frequent visits to the zone. Every day newer methods are being discovered for "tailoring" brainwave patterns and combinations, and eventually we'll know how to "program our brains" to fit the task at hand. And the day may very well come when we all learn to live in the zone, all the time. Considering the amazing computer we carry in our heads, and the great spirit in our hearts and souls, we are certainly capable.

Lifelong Performance Graphs and the Four-Sphere Performance Filter

When it comes to performance, we are not perfect. Our best results, in any activity, don't always show up. We have sensational days, and we have days that are not indicative of our true potential. So if you look at your performances (of *any* activity) as a lifelong graph, you will see ups, downs, and long stretches of "average" performance.

If we were to look back at these graphs at the end of our lives, we could analyze them and pinpoint what kept most of our performances below the levels of our highest potential—the way we performed on those "sensational" days. But how could we have known which missteps we were about to take? If there were just some way that, at the start of an activity, we could eliminate even a *substantial number* of possible "wrong turns," we could come closer to ensuring success. We could set the stage for our best performances. Well, there is a way to do it. It's called a *filter*, more specifically, the *four-sphere performance filter*.

In order to "filter" out elements that could potentially dilute the quality of our focus and resultant performance, we must first define them by examining patterns—patterns of *previous similar attempts*. For example, if you want to have a "parental advice" conversation with your teenager, realizing that these talks often degenerate into a noncommunicative atmosphere, then you might want to examine the mechanics of previous attempts closely. Perhaps your patience begins to wane at the first sign of disagreement, which your ego interprets as rebellion and disrespect. Your resulting anger, which at that point can escalate with minimal provocation, ends all possibility of positive interaction. So upon analyzing the patterns of previous attempts, you are able to define the elements that prevent successful resolution.

Once defined, these elements can then be filtered out of the plan, leaving only the desire for success and letting the light of focus shine on your good intentions.

Pure love, when present before a mirror, is returned in pure form. And good intention, when freed from impurities, cannot be distorted. The four-sphere performance filter removes those impurities and *lets the vibration of good intention massage the moment.* The result is a clear and present positive focus, which is the first step to success. What is this filter? And how is it used?

In order to understand how this filtering process works, we must first take a hard look at the four-sphere model of *integral holistic sequences.* The four territories form a sort of "map of the world." The four spheres represent the true interconnectedness of all major paradigms proposed throughout history. It provides a link, a *possibility* for synthesis.

The four-sphere model is composed of an Upper Left, Upper Right, Lower Left, and Lower Right sector. And every *thing,* every holon (part/whole) in our reality manifests itself in all four domains. The Upper Left represents the individual interior (or the "I," or intentional) domain, the Upper Right the individual exterior (or the "It," or behavioral) domain, the Lower Left the collective interior (or the "We," or cultural) domain, and the Lower Right the collective exterior (or the "We," or social) domain.

The four-sphere model is a very involved, very complex theory, and to go further into it, for our purposes, is not necessary. It is enough for us to say that Spirit manifests in all four spheres, and therefore we must work in awareness of all four: the "I," the "It," and the two "We" domains (collective cultural and collective social).

What does this have to do with the quality of our preparation for performance? We must, in order to proceed with an unpolluted and undistorted plan, cycle our intentions (and their attendant fears) through the four spheres—more specifically, through the I, It, and We domains—so that ego, uncertainty, and service can be treated appropriately, thus freeing up our higher selves to follow our senses and intuition. Let's see how this process works with a practical, everyday example.

Paula was a new sales representative for a large, well-known, industry-leading corporation in Texas. She'd had a similar position with another company but was recruited by a corporate "headhunter," based on her impressive record. After one month in her new job, she was asked by management to give a one-hour talk to a gathering of regional managers on her incredibly successful and innovative sales techniques. What would normally be a very complimentary assignment, however, was obscured by the fact that Paula had a phobia about speaking to groups, and to make matters much worse, this was a group of her new corporate superiors. She literally froze at the thought. The talk was scheduled for the regional meeting in Chicago, in *three weeks!* That evening, at a girls'-night-out dinner party celebrating Paula's new job, one of her best friends gave her a copy of the new book *Exploring the "Zone,"* the exciting new work by Larry Miller with James Redfield, which serves as a practical guide for elevating one's performance in *any* activity. What a timely gift, she thought, a synchronicity of epic proportions!

One week later, Paula had finished the book and her fears had disappeared. In their place stood a plan, based on the innovative techniques she'd learned in the book. She was ready to try them out, under fire. Of the many "performance enhancing" techniques she'd learned in the book, Paula especially liked the *performance filter,* particularly for this situation. So remembering her *previous similar attempts* at speaking before groups, she decided to cycle her fears through the quadrants.

First came the "I" sector. Paula put herself through this quadrant, weighing her *interior* thoughts and emotions regarding public speaking. Having done extremely well in speech and journalism courses in college, she knew that she possessed more than adequate skills and knowledge on the subject. As she reflected on this, it seemed irrational to fear an activity that she had studied and practiced—one whose techniques she had knowledge of. So Paula cleared the hurdle of the "I" domain, *knowing* that she knew how to give a speech.

Then came the "It" domain, the speech itself. Paula had achieved her position in the industry for many reasons. She was bright and attractive, with a charming personality. More importantly, she was extremely articulate, with an extensive and appropriate vocabulary. She could express herself clearly and convincingly. So *writing* a good speech, for her, was a rather simple task. And the subject matter was no problem, given her lofty status on the sales board and her performance-driven rise within the industry. So the "It" (the speech itself) of the holon—her planned activity—was not a problem. She could write a great speech. So now Paula thought, I know that I *know how* to give a speech, and I know how to write a great speech, so the "I" and the "It" are covered; they're no problem at all. But what about the "We"?

This, she now knew, was where the fear resided. So she cycled the *performing* of the speech, in front of other people, through the "We" spheres, the cultural and social. In terms of culture, Paula knew that she would be speaking to people who were no different from her, that their basic business philosophies and histories were similar to her own. There-fore, they were very likely to agree with what she had to say, and they would *understand*. This thought was of great comfort to her. It put her at ease and lifted a great weight of worry from her mind.

And so she turned to the social implications of this speech. These people, she realized, were not adversaries or critics. They were members of the same team, *her* team. They were eager to meet her and hear what she had to say about *their* company, and they were all aware of her record within the industry. These people, she thought, were her staunchest *allies*.

Basically, she would be addressing friends, hardly a situation to be fearful of.   So with her mind at ease, and her fears washed away thanks to the four-sphere cycling technique, Paula proceeded to write the best speech of her life.

But now, she had to actually give the speech! Her preparation and mindset were perfect, and she was ready, until five minutes before the talk. Suddenly, as if delivered from afar, her fears returned as she eyed the room. Her palms began to perspire; her hands began to shake. She wondered if she could remember the words that she'd so skillfully and confidently written. And then Paula remembered another technique from the book, and it fit the situation perfectly: the *pause-button* technique.

So she stopped in her tracks, retreated to the solitude of the hallway, and meditated on some past successes. She recalled, with vivid imagery, the day she locked up the biggest account in the company's history (which revealed her brilliance to upper management) with an impressive and creative sales pitch and closed the deal with her acumen and eloquence. She "heard" the accolades of her boss and co-workers all over again. She experienced the "rush" once more. And she thirsted for that feeling again. So now Paula was armed with complete preparation and fortified by the reversal technique of the pause button, and the momentum, which only minutes before had been decidedly negative, was totally turned around. Paula strode into the room and brought the house down!

Our fears all lie somewhere within the four spheres. The "I," "It," and "We" of every situation provide the breeding ground for performance-eroding worries—worries that prevent us from realizing our strengths and, even more devastating, prevent us from preparing properly. Poor preparation is the absolute main reason for performance failure. *If you prepare completely, you may not win, but you very likely will perform to your potential.* And if you do that, you will very often win.

The four-sphere performance filter—cycling your intentions

(and fears) through the four spheres—will provide you with the freedom to prepare fully, and that is the key. *Preparation is the Tao of performance.*

Many people confuse imagery with *visualization,* but there is a huge difference. Visualization is simply creating mental images. When you visualize something, you are simply picturing it in your mind's eye. But *imagery* is something altogether different, something much more powerful. Imagery adds *sensation* to the mental picture. For example, when you picture your drive sailing down the middle of the fairway, you are visualizing. But when you picture the drive, and then add the *sound* of the club striking the ball, and the *feel* of it, and the "swishing" sound of the club as it moves through the air, and even the sound of the voices of your playing partners saying, "Nice shot," then you are engaging in imagery.

At this point, we want to make an important point about *mental images* and how the mind-body link is made. Image is the lowest and most primitive part of the mind, putting it directly in touch with the highest part of the body. Image, in other words, is the mind's direct connection with the body—its moods, impulses, bioenergy. Our higher concepts, then, can translate downward into simple images, and these have a direct influence on bodily systems, via intention or impulse. In other words, the first stirrings of bodily movement can simply be the reaction to an image.

So now we know that imagery is not just visualizing something. It is adding sensation to the picture, the sounds, the feel, even the smells and tastes of things. This adds greater detail to the image, makes it more real, and strengthens the signal you're sending to the body. *The body will follow the mind's lead, but only if the message is clear and strong.* Here is an example of successful use of imagery.

Bill was in the final match of his club's tennis championship, and he found himself facing match point against a confident opponent, one who had momentum on his side and a big serve that was consistently finding the corners. Everything seemed to be in his opponent's favor, and Bill was definitely reeling and on the ropes. Then Bill suddenly remembered his imagery training.

He quickly stepped away for a few seconds, closed his eyes, and pictured his opponent's serve streaking across the net and landing just where the serves had been landing for the last set and a half. He *heard* his opponent's racquet as it struck the ball and *heard* the ball as it landed on the court. And then he pictured himself making the perfect return, sending the ball back faster than it came, hearing his racquet smash the ball solidly with that unmistakable sound of a well-executed forehand, hearing the grunt of his opponent as he stabbed futilely at the passing ball, and hearing the ball smash against the wall. And then he heard the cheers of the onlookers as they applauded this incredible return.

Then Bill stepped back in, signaling that he was ready. He started his routine for return of service and waited, letting the imagery play out again in his consciousness. In came the serve, and back it went, almost replicating the vivid imagery. Bill avoided match point, experienced a surge of confidence, and proceeded to overwhelm his opponent in short order.

So instead of succumbing to the pressure and folding tent, Bill stopped, hit the pause button, and used imagery to turn his game around. He *rehearsed* his desired result. But for imagery to be successful, it must be *positive imagery,* and it must be *appropriate.*

Performing *positive* imagery, of course, seems like a given. It seems obvious. But it is surprising how many people do just the opposite. Many people, perhaps because of past failures, allow all sorts of negative thoughts to creep in. They expect the worst. And who can blame them, when they've been bitterly disappointed so many times before? You have to *expect* to succeed.

Years ago, a young, really talented college golfer was practicing on the range, and he asked me to watch for a minute. He was striking the ball magnificently; every shot was solid, straight, and long, with the ideal trajectory. His swing was technically sound, and he seemed to be in total control of his shots, with every club. And to top it all off, he was a consistently fine putter, with a better-than-average short game. Eventually, he asked me this question: "I can strike and control the ball as well as anyone. Why do I shoot 72s and 73s, and players who don't hit it nearly as well as I do come in with 68s and 69s?" And I told him, "Because those players *think* that they are going to shoot 69; they *expect* to. You, on the other hand, *think* that you *might* shoot 69. You *hope* to."

You can use imagery all you want to, but you have to expect what you rehearse to happen. You must believe that your picture will develop. I've even used that as a technique, something I call the *Polaroid* technique.

As you construct your mental picture, adding sensation to form vivid positive imagery, you should arrive at a point where you have a very clear image. Now imagine a shutter in your mind that "snaps" that picture. Now envision, in your mind's eye, that "picture" developing, and as it develops and again becomes clear, you continue your preparation for action. This type of clear imagery and visualization, when used as a lead-in to actual performance, is a powerfully effective tool. It "sets the stage" and clears the path for confident action.

The Evolution toward Mindlessness, the Move to Spirit—Developing the Witness

The Great Chain (or Nest) of Being follows the progression of matter, life, mind, soul, and spirit. To progress from one level to a higher one involves transcending the lower level while including it in the new, emerging one. Transcend and include—the way of evolution.

When we experience the higher states—when we get a glimpse—we spring free from the workings of the mind and its constant companion, the ego. We enter a sort of "mindless" state where instinct takes over from ego, and our natural gifts are prominently displayed. But these displays, unfortunately, are short-lived, as the "noise" and attachments of the world get through.

Through diligent "Witness development" practice, however, we can prolong our visits to these higher places and begin to minimize the power of the ego. *As we feed the Witness with the nutrient of diligent practice, we will see the ego shrink.* This "Witness development" is a contemplative, perhaps meditative practice where you ask, "Who is looking at the wall?", and then, "Who is it that is *wondering* who is looking at the wall?", and on and on. As this goes along, the deeper you get into this "endless mirror" type of contemplation, the closer you get to the ultimate Witness, the essence of Spirit. It takes your mind away—far away—from the surface ego that calls most of the shots, most of the time.

Living only through the ego is a very whimsical, ungrounded situation that many times ends with regret, unless it feeds the ego of someone who needs our energy. And then he *owes* us and gives us some as payback. This give and take of energy always leaves one side lacking, and the debt weighs heavily on the depleted one. Our Essence-Witness should at all times be a "guardian at the door," watching who comes and goes—the various personalities of ego—until it is strengthened enough to stand alone, and no one else comes.

CHAPTER 3

The Celestine Insights
and the Zone

When *The Celestine Prophecy* was first published, it brought the reality of an already existent spiritual awakening to the world's consciousness. Through the Insights revealed in *The Celestine Prophecy,* millions became familiar with words and concepts such as *synchronicity* and *interconnectedness,* and they learned of the power of conscious energy. And due to the widespread popularity of the book, and the feelings of association that it provoked in its readers, the wave of consciousness rolling across the globe gathered steam as the move toward critical mass accelerated.

The Insights, "The Celestine Insights," laid out for all to see the progression of this move toward what has been called "enlightenment," or the "ultimate" step in spiritual evolution. Enlightenment has been called many things and described in many ways, but what it really is, regardless of the whimsical constructs of language, is an encounter with the deepest level of reality, the baseline of energy. It is the master tape of reality. At this level, there is no dilution due to the "branching out" into level after level of infinite generations. This level is pure essence.

In today's particular language, describing what is thought to be *the mysterious phenomenon of spontaneous excellence,* this place is called the "zone." It could be called the manifestation of the highest potential of any phenomenon or any activity. Getting a taste of this potential—this connection to the Divine that we all long for—seems random and mysteriously elusive, and most consider it to be an accidental occurrence.

This book, *Exploring the "Zone,"* shows that the "zone" is not at all accidental, that it is the natural state of things, and that its mystery and wonder lie hidden just beneath the thick crust of the constructs of the ego, the veils of the mind.

The Celestine Insights could well be called "steps to the zone," as they take us on an *ascending* journey of consciousness, a journey into finer and finer dimensions of mind and body. These steps—the Insights—are cultural signposts on the way to The One. Let's take a look at these steps, keeping in mind that each recognition, each intuition, and each synchronicity that occurs is a clear sign of the transformation of the substances of our very being.

The First Insight

> The First Insight says that a new spiritual awakening is occurring in human culture, an awakening brought about by a critical mass of individuals who experience their lives as a spiritual unfolding, a journey in which we are led forward by mysterious coincidences.

It's no wonder that zone experiences seem completely random and accidental to people who have not felt a spiritual stirring—people who have not yet begun to "work on themselves" consciously. Spiritually, as well as consciously, these people are still asleep and have not begun the transformation process. They experience little synchronicity and even fail to recognize occurrences of it. Their experiences remain on a completely physical level, and they remain in this spiritual holding pattern until some event "pops" them open, like a dormant kernel awaiting a certain heat—a certain stimulation.

The stimulation—the heat—can come in a variety of forms: a book they read, a friend who influences them, or a tragic life event. Sometimes the awakening can be the result of a devastating failure or of a monumentally life changing joyous event, such as long-awaited success, the birth of a child, or falling in love. Because these people are not yet open to the revelations that synchronicities (meaningful coincidences) can bring, and especially because the antennas of their senses are not "fully raised," they remain unaware of possibilities that are constantly parading before them. As a result, "gateways" to elevated performance—and "zone" experiences—go unnoticed.

Higher states of functioning require higher states of awareness. And when the senses are enhanced, we receive more signals, and clearer signals. More options are presented. The result is a more efficient functioning of the entire organism. Diminished signal reception means fewer options for action, and so performance slows to a more baseline, mechanistic mode with little creativity. There is no innovation and slow evolution.

So in order to begin a move toward elevating one's efficiency, in any area of one's life, it is first necessary to realize that there *are* greater potentials, and that the current operational level is below those possibilities. It's the spark of realization that elicits change.

When this spark ignites us, things start happening. We become more attuned to our surroundings, more aware. Our antennas go up. Synchronicities start occurring more often, and they often become more astounding.

Sometimes, due to a mostly accidental alignment of many factors, we stumble into the "zone." The experiences are vivid, so different from the norm, but they are fleeting and temporary.

Because we are not rooted in a higher place, we are not anchored in the zone. And so the glimpses come infrequently and without warning. This "stumbling into a higher place" happens when one or a combination of elements of the zone is present, and when our senses or emotions are heightened.

The catalyst for this can be a beautiful place, it could be that first cool day of fall, or it could be having a great time with wonderful friends. Things and circumstances like this can catapult us onto the doorstep of higher states, and there we become fertile fields for the seeds of transformation. So the First Insight, we might say, is where we "pop open," stirred from our sleep by a sudden, often unexpected stimulus.

The Second Insight

> The Second Insight states that this awakening represents the creation of a new, more complete worldview, which replaces a 500-year-old preoccupation with secular survival and comfort. While this technological preoccupation was an important step, our awakening to life's coincidences is opening us up to the real purpose of human life on this planet, and the real nature of our universe.

When we are mired in narcissism, tending to the demanding and unceasing whims of the ego, our possibilities are limited. But when we broaden our view and work as allies with others and the world around us, doors fly open. While technological advance creates a better life in many ways, it tends little to the emotional and spiritual needs of "us"—the ones who benefit from that technology.

There must be a balance, a balance of what the modern philosopher Ken Wilber calls "sense and soul," and our collective and individual quest for that balance has begun as a result of the unconscious restlessness that began surfacing decades ago. As this quest progresses, we not only realize a more complete worldview, we become more complete individuals, and more complete individuals result in more complete societies and a healthier, happier world.

"Peace, Brother," the anthem of the sixties, was the primordial scream for this quest for balance. And when your kernel "pops," and your personal quest for balance of sense and soul begins, your contribution to the collective effort is made. You can't minimize the importance of this contribution—for you and for the world.

Until *your* worldview expands, you will remain out of balance and confined to the limited spaces of the ego. All the magic will stay out of your reach, and the zone, for you, will remain a mystery.

The Third Insight

The Second Insight, *the broadening of our view*, leads to the third, and to the next step along the pathway to the zone. We now experience that we live not in a material universe, but in a universe of dynamic energy. Everything extant is a field of sacred energy that we can sense and intuit. Moreover, we humans can project our energy by focusing our attention in the desired direction (*where attention goes, energy flows*), influencing other energy systems and increasing the pace of coincidences in our lives.

Viewing the universe as an energy field is nothing new, of course. In fact, modern science inches closer all the time to purporting this view as scientific fact, and the day is nearing when empirical, measurable data will publicly support it. Already, privately, most scientists know this view to be fact and know that it is the true nature of reality.

All matter is ultimately nothing more than vibrating energy fields, made up of the same substances (all energy) in different combinations and configurations. The book you're holding in your hand is made of the same materials as your hand, only in different combinations. These different combinations account for the differences in appearance, texture, densities, and hence rates of vibration. They are of different frequencies.

As matter becomes more dense, or more "solid," it slows in rate of vibration (frequency). A rock, for instance, could be called "frozen energy."

As we move up the vibratory ladder, frequencies increase. Matter becomes *finer*. As we (as matter) become more conscious, more aware of and open to an expanded worldview, we too become finer, literally, as the combinations of substances that comprise us change.

We increase in vibratory rate as we move up the ladder toward the Absolute—toward the zone. It's why the saints, masters, and yogis, from every tradition and discipline, are depicted throughout historical literature as light, sometimes even levitating, indicative of the lightness they achieved due to their extreme self-development. Their energies are of a very refined nature.

Looking at the world in this way—at its true nature— changes everything. It changes the perception of and the ramifications of our intended actions. We realize that we are not separate from the world around us, that we are part of a vast, interconnected web of *available* energy, and that every part of this web influences, in some way, every other part.

Most of us have always thought the mind (and thoughts) to be some ethereal, mysterious domain, not part and parcel of the physical body. But that is not the case (see Candace Pert's book, *Molecules of Emotion: Why You Feel the Way You Feel,* the cutting-edge, scientific work on this subject). *Thought energy* is the same (and as "real") as any other form of energy, but in different form. This energy can be collected, concentrated, directed, minimized, or maximized. And tragically, it can be ignored.

We've all used thought energy many times, and have even sometimes known the results of its power, when we've prayed, or wished for something with "all our might."

This Insight, the realization of how energy forms the fabric of our world, is a biggie. It's a springboard to conscious development, and it represents the first big change in the configuration of the energy fields that weave and oscillate throughout the form that we call "ourselves."

Once we realize that we have the power to focus and direct our energy, and that the intention of that "beam" can influence other, even distant energy systems, we've taken a giant step toward achieving the reality of higher states of functioning. We see obstacles as nothing more than other energy systems, systems that we can interact with. In this way, we can shift from an adversarial view to a collaborative one, and from that vantage point transformational results can occur. This view raises energy levels, while seeing obstacles as insurmountable roadblocks lowers energy.

High energy invites development, while low energy impedes it.

If you're looking for zone experiences through the thickened lens of the flatland empiricist, you're in for a futile search. But if you see the true nature of yourself and the world around you, a world of wondrous possibility opens, every minute of every day.

The Fourth Insight

> Too often, humans cut themselves off from the greater source of this energy and so feel weak and insecure. To gain energy we tend to manipulate or force others to give us attention and thus energy. When we successfully dominate others in this way, we feel more powerful, but they are left weakened and often fight back. Competition for scarce, human energy is the cause of all conflict between people.

This conflict, so prevalent that it consumes virtually all of our effort, is one of the primary reasons that higher states of functioning remain out of reach for most people. Their time and available energy are spent trying to compete for some form of energy in order to feed their low supplies. These attempts at "energy theft" can take many forms.

These people seek attention in various ways, some very harmful. They belittle and criticize others in order to build *themselves* up. They seek temporary gratification with drugs, sex, and illegal activity, thinking that the brief "high" or thrill will bolster their energies. Or they may engage in dangerous risk-taking activity, believing that the notoriety they achieve will make them "important." But mostly they do whatever it takes to "suck" energy from others in order to fill their empty reservoirs.

All of these efforts keep them mired in the depths of nonproductiveness, and they never give themselves the chance to tap into the limitless energy that literally fills the world around them. When we stop vying for the energy of others, and seek it in the limitless field around us, we make available to ourselves the great power and tremendous energies of the universe. Instead of dwelling on the faults and shortcomings of others, if we bind with powerful, established energy systems (such as 300-year-old oak trees), our own energy systems are uplifted rather than torn down. This ascending scale of energy is what brings us to higher states, while *descending energy acts* (acts that fly in the face of conscience) slow us down to the point of nonproductiveness. Cutting-edge research shows that there is a correlation between low energy states and physical and mental disease.

Setting the stage for zone experiences requires connection to finer energies. Through this connection, our own energies are raised. Only acts that are conducive to such connections should be considered, and ones that are detrimental—ones that have the opposite potential—should be avoided. With habitual employment of such discernment, there is a constant up-flow of energy, the senses are sharpened, and actions are efficient, often extraordinary.

The Fifth Insight

Insecurity and violence ends when we experience a connection with divine energy within, a connection described by mystics of all traditions. A sense of lightness—buoyancy—along with the constant sensation of love are measures of this connection. If these measures are present, the connection is real. If not, it is only pretended.

Watch little children at play, and see the "spring in their step." In their obvious state of joy and wonder, pure love is there in abundance. It's another example of what the appearance of the ego and its narcissistic development does to us. We lose that joy and wonder, that love connection. We stop *gawking* at the world and its many wonders, the way that only little children do.

It is our quest, as life-hardened adults, to return to that joyful, innocent state. But it seems we cannot. The ego appears, we get older and accumulate life experiences, and we develop an array of false personalities—a different manifestation for each situation. Along the way, that love connection is lost in a ocean of fears, hurts, and sadness.

But that connection is still there, and so is the joy and wonder. Every now and then, something happens—a certain song, a little child, a new love, or a touching gesture from an old one—and there's that feeling again, that connection. The first clear, clean day of spring can bring a spring to the step, a feeling of lightness. It's the heart that gives us lightness. *When the heart is heavy, the mind must carry the burden.* And the mind is very weak.

The mind is built on the fragile, shifting sands of the ego, while the heart is eternally and firmly anchored on the sea of infinite love. That's why we must always strive to "follow our hearts," for the heart never lies. But the mind, with its attendant ego, cannot tell us the truth.

Until the quest begins to find the way back to essence, love, and total honesty, and to strip away the layers of "personalities" that the ego has constructed to deal with its never-ending network of lies, that connection to love—and that feeling of lightness—cannot be made. And that state of the innocent child, that magical state of the zone, will remain elusive. Visits will be accidental, fleeting, and infrequent.

The Sixth Insight

The more we stay connected, the more we are acutely aware of those times when we lose connection, usually when we are under stress. In these times, we can see our own particular way of stealing energy from others. Once our manipulations are brought to personal awareness, our connection becomes more constant and we can discover our own growth path in life, and our spiritual mission—the personal way we can contribute to the world.

It's a matter of, as the modern sports psychologists say, "staying focused," and they just don't know how right they are! The focus must remain, for as long as possible, on our innate connection to the unbroken field of universal energy. To that energy, our essences, our hearts, are infinitely connected.

The only thing that can (and constantly does) break that connection is the ego—the harmful constructs of the mind. Why we even have this "ego," this "albatross around our necks," is a matter for long discussion, and there is no need to get into so esoteric a matter here. What we want to focus on is how to disentangle from its grasp.

We constantly have to monitor ourselves, keep watch on the ego. And that seemingly simple statement is very profound, for when we say, "monitor ourselves," the question becomes, "*who* is doing the monitoring when we monitor ourselves?" The answer is that the *essence,* the *heart,* the part of us that operates from *objective conscience,* is doing the monitoring. That part is called the Witness. The Witness just steps back and observes the ego at work. It watches the parade of personalities come and go. It just *observes.* And the longer it observes, the stronger it becomes, and the stronger it becomes, the weaker the ego grows.

When you're engaged in any activity, remember to call on the Witness, and let it step back and watch. As you strengthen the Witness, you draw closer to the "zone." Witness meditation has long been one of the most popular forms of meditation in esoteric disciplines, because these serious practitioners recognize the tremendous value of its effects. Later, when we discuss the Eleventh Insight, the one that led us into the new millennium, we will explore in depth the ultimate goal (and reward) of the fervent practice of Witness meditation.

So once we acquire the feeling of being connected to the world around us, however fleeting that feeling may be, we must constantly try to remember that connection, that feeling. This is what Gurdjieff meant by his famous mantra, "Remember yourselves, everywhere and in everything." If you just go along in a sleepwalking state, like a machine, subject to mechanical law, and at the mercy of the ego, the *self* can't *do* anything. The ego and its never-satisfied personalities make all the decisions.

But if you constantly remember your ever-present connection to the Divine—the One Source—then your true self, your "I," *the Witness,* will flourish and nourish your life. And all of your actions will be pure, unfiltered, and free from the contamination of the self-serving ego. The more you rest in the Witness, the longer your connection to the zone.

The Seventh Insight

> Knowing our personal mission further enhances the flow of mysterious coincidences as we are guided toward our destinies. First we have a question; then dreams, daydreams, and intuitions lead us toward the answers, which usually are synchronistically provided by the wisdom of another human being. It's a well-known phrase: "When the student is ready, the master appears."

As awakening proceeds, we begin to clarify our life direction. *We take a path.* The path may take many forms. It could be a new way of living with regard to personal caretaking (exercise, diet, cosmetic surgery), it could be a change in profession, or it could be educational or recreational. It could be a big change in one's social life (marriage, divorce, the decision to have a child, or not to). But this shift is featured by a new clarity, a new certainty about our life mission and purpose, a certainty of *who we are.*

As we embark down this new path, filled with a sense of purpose, excitement, and curiosity (reminiscent of the joy and wonder of childhood), synchronicities abound. We meet just the right person at just the right time. We make connections that advance our march toward our goals. And we find mentors who add wisdom and knowledge to our mission.

We begin to use our intuition for all decisions (we follow our hearts), and disregard the transparent dictates of the ego, and we begin, due to our self-remembering, to see through the empty facade of our false personalities. We are, at this point, reaching a state of balance, as the reemerging essence begins to replace the ever-shrinking ego. The zone is becoming less mysterious and more *possible.*

Regarding mentors, there are two schools of thought. The first says that in choosing a mentor, one should check his lineage to see what schools of thought shaped his present way of teaching or thinking. In other words, find out who the mentor's mentor is or was. The second school says that it is the connection to the mentor that is felt that is the important factor. When the intuitive connection is felt, then the teachings will follow in appropriate fashion. The mentor serves as an inspiration, and as a perfect mirror, reflecting back your higher self through his eyes.

The Eighth Insight

> We can increase the frequency of guiding coincidences by uplifting every person who comes into our lives. Care must be taken not to lose our inner connection in romantic relationships. Uplifting others is especially effective in groups where each member can feel the energy of all the others. With children it is extremely important for their early security and growth. By seeing the beauty in every face, we lift others into their wisest selves and increase the chances of hearing a synchronistic message.

It's like gift giving, where the act of giving your feelings for someone in the form of a material gift or an unrequested good deed (*random acts of kindness*) lifts you higher. When this concept is practiced with all sentient beings, the energy of your world is raised and multiplied. And when the energy of your world increases, you operate in a clear, coherent field, and miracles happen. Important connections are made, and paths of action become crystal clear.

When you follow the lead of the increasing number of coincidences in your life, you come to see that you are being guided toward your life mission. When you surrender to synchronicity's loving embrace, you are swept away in a torrent of intuition and divine connection. Your heart tells you just where to go and just what to do.

Conversely, when the ego rules, all energies stay mired in the lowly state of narcissism, and in this low energy field, nothing opens. The door to synchronicities remains shut, and we are led only in circles by the ego as it chases its own tail. It is an endless loop of chaos and confusion.

In the beginning of a romantic relationship, the partners marvel at how much they have in common. Their frequencies are so close that they literally resonate in all that they do, all that they say. As the relationship goes on, if this resonance is not frequently reinforced, it can drift apart, gaps can occur and widen, until ultimately the frequencies become nonsynchronous and the partners find themselves worlds apart, wondering where the magic went. They seem now to have nothing in common, the lines of communication between them shut down, and they find themselves in that all-too-familiar position (in today's world) of being *alone together.*

Couples who evolve together, that is, "work on themselves" and develop consciously together, don't seem to have that problem, because they go up the scale of development at the same rate, at the same time, together. And couples who have had long, happy lives together even take on similar physical characteristics and tend to think and say the same things at the same time. It's yet another example of how the many constantly try to return to and become The One.

When members of a group consciously raise their levels of energy, the energy of the whole group can be raised. Just witness a sports team that suddenly "catches fire" because of an inspirational, passionate burst of performance by one of its members. One person can change the entire momentum of a team with inspired play, especially when that team or group is committed to and focused upon a common, cherished goal.

It is vitally important for us, as parents, to help keep the energy of our children at high levels, to uplift them constantly, particularly in times of frustration. We have to teach them always to operate in "the now" and focus on their assets and positive traits. And we have to teach them the importance of uplifting others, for it is within that framework that their own esteem is solidly constructed.

We have a unique opportunity with our children, even a moral responsibility, to get them started in life in the right direction, the direction that leads to conscious development. With such a start, they can avoid the ego buildup that eventually leads to the obliteration of essence, a state from which they may never recover.

They should be made aware, early on, of the nature of synchronicities, how to stay open to them, and how to follow their clues. If they develop these habits early, they will experience many more moments in the glow of their highest potentials. The zone, for them, will be accessible most of the time. This gift to our children—to teach them to live consciously—can be our greatest contribution to our own evolution as a species.

The Ninth Insight

As we all evolve toward the best completion of our spiritual missions, the technological means of survival will be fully automated as humans focus instead on synchronistic growth. Such growth will move humans into higher energy states, ultimately transforming our bodies into spiritual form and uniting this dimension of existence with the afterlife dimension, ending the cycle of birth and death.

We humans, for a long time, have been devoted to the goal of technological advance. And we have done an amazing job of improving all of the *things* around us—but at a price. In the process of working to improve everything around us, we overlooked working to improve ourselves.

As a result, the inhabitants of this glittering world murder and steal, burn their minds and bodies with drugs, abandon and abuse children, and tear apart their own families. They lie as a way of life, plunder energy without remorse, and pillage the Earth in every way conceivable. They start wars, riot against all authority, and refuse to search out positive change.

But the wave of consciousness rolling across the planet is taking dead aim and is poised to awaken the sleeping masses, one by one. People are, in record numbers, working on themselves, developing consciously, improving their various centers simultaneously. The momentum is such that a critical mass is inevitable, and already, in the new millennium, there are visible signs of rising energy.

The day will come, as the "soul age" advances, when the fragile film of organic life on Earth strengthens and refines in unison to higher vibratory levels. The transformation of the substances of being will move in the direction of an ascending evolutionary octave—toward spiritual form—and toward The One. And when the transformation is complete, and "man" looks back at his often painful history, he will see that his highest expression was always right there inside of him, just out of reach. There were glimpses, but the veils were thick and many.

What we call the zone has always been our home.

When you get a small, brief taste of it, when you experience one of those "white moments," then you know what it's like to *be* the world, instead of being *in* it.

The Tenth Insight

The Tenth Insight is the realization that throughout history human beings have been unconsciously struggling to implement this lived spirituality on Earth. Each of us comes here on assignment, and as we pull this understanding into consciousness, we can remember a fuller birth vision of what we wanted to accomplish with our lives. Furthermore, we can remember a common world vision of how we will all work together to create a new spiritual culture. We know that our challenge is to hold this vision with intention and prayer every day.

As the world population rapidly increased, it became necessary, and at times even urgent, to create technological advances in order to accommodate and service the growth. And while we were immersed in the search for these advances, spiritual matters were relegated to the depths of our consciousness. But they were always there, just below the waves, bubbling up at various times throughout history on the influence of saints and mystics.

During the last third of the twentieth century, the bubbles came up again, this time manifesting in art expression, social turmoil, and an obsessive desire for peace, the latter triggered by unprecedented acts of violence in every corner of the world. And then there were the "evolutionary scouts," the writers and thinkers who brought to the world, in highly visible works, the reality of a new possibility and the chance for transformation. As the century ended, and a new one—and a new millennium—began, there is a renewed sense of expectation that the spiritual trend will continue, and perhaps usher in a new age, the Soul Age.

While technological advance must and will continue, it must occur in conjunction with the search for spirit in each of us. It is a unique chance, one that may not come again, and it is up to each of us to hold the vision of the emerging spirituality.

Bookshelves are lined with self-help books. Philosophy, psychology, and "new age" sections in bookstores hold unprecedented inventories. Conversations about self-development, "working on oneself," and spirituality can be heard in every place that people congregate, and classes, seminars, and computer chat-room forums abound on the subject. People have had enough of the "focus on technology" mindset. They want to pay attention to themselves for a change instead of a mechanical invention, and particularly to that part of themselves that they believe can be immortal.

The power of prayer has become more prevalent in our consciousness, thanks in part to the exciting new research on the subject, particularly in the writings of Dr. Larry Dossey. And the power of intention, or "thought energy," is practiced by more and more people every day, all around the world. The youngsters of today, the *Children of the New Millennium,* are more "tuned in" to consciousness and spirituality than any other generation in history, as they've come on to the scene in the midst of this global awakening. It will be their mission to accelerate the evolution of consciousness on this planet and "supervise" the work we've begun.

Tiger Woods, at a young age, continues to set records in the world of professional golf. His visit to the zone has been an extraordinarily long one, but it's no surprise. Tiger was raised in an atmosphere of Eastern tradition and thought, and his "thought energy" was well developed at a young age. The twenty-first century will see many more people like Tiger Woods, consciously developed, intuitive, creative beyond the norm, and blessed with a full arsenal of natural gifts. Special people who come along—like Tiger Woods—help us all to *hold the vision* of our higher potentials.

The Eleventh Insight

The Eleventh Insight is the precise method through which we hold the vision. For centuries, religious scriptures, poems, and philosophies have pointed to a latent power of mind within all of us that mysteriously helps to affect what occurs in the future. It has been called faith power, positive thinking, or the power of prayer. We are now taking this power seriously enough to bring a fuller knowledge of it into public awareness. We are finding that this prayer power is a field of intention and moves out from us and can be extended and strengthened, especially when we connect with others in a common vision. This is the power through which we hold the vision of a spiritual world and build the energy in ourselves and others to make this vision a reality.

Now we come to the doorstep of the zone. The power of intention, and the power of expectation, clear the path to that mysterious phenomenon of spontaneous excellence, that connection with the "grand design."

Everything in the universe is energy, including ourselves, and it is the *management of energy* that determines the result of all actions. Of particular importance is the transmutation of negative energy, for it not only redirects wasted energy to an ascending trajectory, but it increases the influence of intention and expectation, the "power lines" of energy projection.

One of the exciting things about the consciousness movement is the fact that *energy management* tends to multiply among those who practice it. Intentions and expectations create "feeding frenzies" of energy projectionists, all benefiting from each one's attempts at energy management.

If you examine the actions of people who have zone experiences on a regular basis (winners, "lucky" or successful people, etc.), you'll find that they have several things in common. They are often strong-minded people, that is, people who can focus fully on the task at hand. As a result, their beams of intentions—their thought energies—are pure and strong. Comfortable in that knowledge, they *expect* positive results. And they almost always get them.

Imagine a world where everyone, using the power of intention, offers only prayer to others, and becomes to them a mirror in which they see their perfect selves. And imagine a world where the power of positive expectation rules, laying out pathways on which thought energy can travel to and interact with other equally powerful fields of clear intention. When we reach these stages in the Soul Age, we will reconstruct reality to match the perfect design that has always been at our essence.

As we accelerate into the new millennium, we need only to remind ourselves to hold the vision of our possible—and inevitable—future.

The Two Streams of Human Life

At a certain point in the evolution of mankind (around the Babylonian era), there became "two streams" of human life. One stream, the *mainstream,* can be called the *psychostatic society,* the other the *psychokinetic society.* The psychostatic society refers to the masses. And this sector is characterized by what G. I. Gurdjieff called "waking sleep."

These people do not work on themselves consciously. They are only machines, carried along by circumstance. They are, in every sense, *mechanical.* The psychokinetic society, however, does consciously work toward development as a being who can *do*—one who has a *will.*

The problem is that all of those in power are the leaders of the psychostatic society, and despite efforts of the psychokinetic community to influence mainstream thinking and action, little influence is realized. It is the mission of a book like this to attempt to find a way to solve this problem. If the unconscious of the world would follow the lead of the conscious, the mantle of power would vanish into the nothingness that it really is, in terms of infinity.

How can the Earth develop its soul when the bulk of its conscious energy (the unconscious masses) is in arrested development? One wonders what influence it would take at this point—given the sheer numbers of the unconscious masses—to shift the psychostatic stream over. What bridge can span the gap? You have to wonder—when you watch the news at night—if even divine intervention would be enough.

And yet, every good person knows that every day there are thousands of "good news" stories out there, unsung heroes in every city and town in the world. These acts easily eclipse the news we see, the news that is bad enough, shocking enough, to be worthy of airtime to the masses.

Why do the power people, the people of the media and the advertisement industry, want to keep the human spirit down by selecting low-energy news? The answer: they are, themselves, basically low-energy forms whose only desired "food" is more power over the masses. As long as the masses remain uninspired and uninformed of the possibility of further conscious development, they remain subdued, suppressed, and subservient to those in power.

The "power people," the leaders of the psychostatic society, survive and thrive by "sucking" energy from the masses they control. But their destiny is sealed by their failure to develop the substance of a soul, and their only acquired and developed substance—power—vanishes with their own ashes. Again the question begs for an answer: *What bridge can span the gap?*

We refer once more to the wave of consciousness rolling across the planet. While undeniably growing, gathering steam, and expanding to every part of the globe, it remains stunted by massive opposition. For every new member of the psychokinetic society, there is born into our troubled and overpopulated inner cities 500 future members of the psychostatics, and that ratio is likely to continue until that bridge is found.

We can look to the Internet, with its incredible ability to mass communicate. We can look to the appearance of a bold conscious leader, if we can find one. Or we can all step up efforts to spread the words of Jesus and the other Messengers who have appeared all throughout history in attempts to awaken the masses.

The messages of the mystics have endured, but many in all too esoteric forms. One thing appears certain: We must lead the masses to that bridge while they are young, before they are irrevocably lost. We must reach the children with the message of consciousness, and see that their development is monitored carefully and reinforced daily.

Their education, along with the acquisition of general and functional knowledge, must include *conscious work on themselves* as well as *consciousness studies*. At an early age, before spoilage at the altar of greed, they must learn in their minds what their hearts already know—that what really matters is the development of the soul of every living thing. It's the only way out of the endless loop. It's the only way to *real* freedom.

Training Away Our Natural Gifts

Several years ago, while developing some of the theories that led to the publication of *Holographic Golf,* I tried an experiment with children that yielded revealing results. I would take a youngster who had never swung a golf club, give him a seven iron and a golf ball, place him in a field with a flagstick and a hole, and situate him about 150 yards away from the flag. I would explain that the object was, using only the club, to get the ball into the hole in as few "hits" (strokes) as possible, and I would tell him nothing else—not how to hold the club, how to stand, or anything else. I would inform him that I'd return in a half-hour to see how he was doing. And I would leave him, go into the woods, hide in the trees, and observe him with binoculars.

The first few attempts by these kids were what you'd expect: awkward swipes and hatchetlike slashes at the ball, grips of every type (none correct), stances of every kind, and strange postures. But then they would begin to figure it out, how to propel the ball forward most efficiently. As the process evolved, their form would become more conventional and effective as they refined their methods on their own, using for reference only their natural instincts. At the end of the sessions an amazing picture had developed. They had created a method for propelling the ball forward that very closely resembled a pretty good golf swing, all on their own.

After witnessing this same scenario over and over again, I became convinced that people who say that the golf swing is not a natural movement are wrong. What *is* unnatural is when those same boys and girls start taking golf lessons from a "teacher," learn the *mechanics* of the golf swing, and proceed, through a long, analytical process, to tie themselves up in knots, losing all sense of their natural instincts, feel, and rhythm along the way. The "teacher," through an endless series of positions and swing mechanics, has helped them to "train away" their natural gifts.

Many world-class players have fallen into the same trap from time to time. One shining example is Hal Sutton, one of the world's top-ranked players, who nearly wrecked his career by trying to develop the "perfect" swing. Only when, in a desperate state, he decided to forget all of the mechanics and just go back to swinging his natural, instinctive way did he regain the form that had brought him early success.

It's a lesson well worth remembering. Trust your instincts and use your natural rhythm. And *never make the mistake of training away your natural gifts* through over-analysis. Don't view every bad shot as evidence of a *flaw*—view each simply as a mistake. If there was an intrinsic flaw, you would *never* hit top-quality shots. Realize the mistake, take a corrective preview swing, and try again, with the same intended technique and with your natural rhythm.

The Mind: The Myths of Its Power

Much has been written about the mind-body connection, suggesting that the mind can control the actions of the body, and it is even implied that the body can be influenced in positive ways by specific "mental techniques." Still today, even in the face of contradictory scientific evidence, bookshelves are lined with volume after volume of these "mind-body" books. The reality is that enhanced states of human performance (the zone) occur when one "loses his mind," that is, functions physically from *instinct* and *reaction to sensory input,* and that in fact activity of the mind is only a deterrent to such states.

When the physical body simply reacts, instinctively, to sensory data, with the mind simply witnessing the action, it reacts appropriately and immediately. But when the mind tries to analyze that data, and especially when it overanalyzes it, the information becomes distorted by considerations of the ego, and the subsequent physical response is a response to that distortion. Earlier we saw that it is common for modern man to "train away his natural gifts," through piecemeal observation and dissection of what should be a flowing, spontaneous experience.

The advent of the video camera, with its stop action and frame-by-frame capability, has been both a blessing and a curse for today's athlete. It is a blessing for its diagnostic potential (valuable to the teacher, if used properly) and a curse for the student, who can use it ad nauseam to pick apart his technique. The teacher should never show stop or frame-by-frame action to the student, for it invites overanalysis and isolates only part of what is a connected, flowing whole.

The teacher can use it for diagnostic purposes—like an x-ray to the physician—and determine where the whole is breaking down. He can then take measures to correct things that, in the chain reaction, are negatively affecting the flow of the entire motion.

When a student, who does not possess the knowledge of a real teacher, attempts to isolate a specific fault, extract it from the motion, fix it, and reinsert it, it cannot work. Knowledge of the entire motion—and the chain reaction of causes and effects—is necessary in order to take effective steps.

Every world-class athlete reports that when he is operating at high levels of efficiency, when he is "in the zone," he is thinking of nothing. But ask him what he's thinking about when he is performing poorly, or in a slump, and he will tell you that he is thinking of every conceivable detail of his technique. He is analyzing and experimenting, immersed in mechanics, and overworking the mind.

Always remember, in everything that you do, to trust your instincts, *your feelings.* Try not to train away your natural gifts.

The Power of Pairs

For centuries, man has sought enlightenment—liberation from the ego—in a multitude of ways. Employing practices from every known tradition in his attempts to get to the "next level," he has chased the mystery inexhaustibly.

In the book *Altered States of Consciousness,* a classic edited by Charles Tart, there is a chapter written by Tart himself entitled "Psychedelic Experiences Associated with a Novel Hypnotic Procedure, *Mutual Hypnosis.*" In 1962, Tart conducted an experiment to test out the hypotheses that psychedelic experiences could be produced through hypnosis and that depth of trance could be increased with training. These hypotheses flew in the face of certain other research.

Specifically, Tart wanted to test the effect of "rapport," the harmony and equanimity that exist in the communication between speaker and listener, on the hypnotic process. The method he used was to have *two people simultaneously fill the roles of both hypnotist and hypnotized,* a process he called *mutual hypnosis.* Tart had "A" hypnotize "B," and when in a hypnotized state, "B" would hypnotize "A." When "A" was also hypnotized, he or she would deepen the trance state of "B," who would then deepen "A"'s trance, and so on. Tart reasoned that a deep level of rapport would thus develop. Graduate psychology students were used in the experiments.

The results were astounding and confirmed Tart's theories. The subjects reported *ever-increasing depths of trance, shared dreams, a sense of merging identities,* and *a partial blending of themselves quite beyond the degree of contact human beings expect to share with each other.* In their shared dreams, they saw and experienced things that they both described as "what you might think of as heaven."

There is an incredible book called *Joshua's Way,* written by Robert P. Baker, that goes deeply into Tart's ideas and expands on them. It is a cutting-edge work and, though little known now, is surely destined to receive the recognition it deserves for its "ahead of its time" nature.

To set the stage for seeing how the power of pairs might help unlock the mysteries, let's look at some real results of esoteric studies. We refer to a great discussion *Joshua's Way* has about these ideas:

> All things gravitate toward being like their neighbor. Hot and cold air meet and their temperatures eventually drift toward that of the other, storm or no storm. Ice and hot water seek to become alike in their temperature. We have long known that women in the same proximity eventually have their menstrual cycles together. Live cells from two hearts placed so that they touch on the same slide under a microscope beat together. Even

inanimate grandfather clocks have been known to swing their pendulums in synchrony when placed close to one another. Energy seeks to be in harmony with surrounding energy as though it is trying to unite, to be the same, to become one.

Studies at the Stanford Research Institute have demonstrated conclusively that some people, while focusing upon another, can "see" what that other person can actually see, even though they may be great distances apart. Additional studies showed that two people could synchronize their brainwave patterns. When one begins to focus upon the other, that person begins to entrain or synchronize their brainwaves with that of the other. The implications are profound. It explains why friends and lovers often know each other's thoughts.

Identical twins are naturally entrained, so it is clear why one can often know precisely what is going on with the other, even when in different locations.

When one is in love, the other is almost constantly in focus; therefore, entraining occurs.

One begins to develop the same brainwave pattern as the other. Of course, each entrains upon the other; so, in some measure, you are entraining upon your own pattern. After a while, it is likely there is only one brainwave pattern manifested in two individuals. Therefore, love sickness and infatuation result, in part, from the loss of personal awareness and identity as the two merge deeper into their own experience, for the more they look at the other, the more they see themselves. It is as though they are looking into a hall of mirrors that goes on forever. Unwittingly, we become Narcissus looking at our own reflection in the pool, except that here the pool is the eyes of our beloved. The emotional experience of that love is profound and often generalizes to all things, to everyone, and all of life. It is the ultimate feeling of love and connectedness with all things.

But this type of love wields a power beyond the capacity of the human mind and body to hold. Like electricity going through a fuse, the currents will get too strong. Love, especially romantic love, hits resistance within the human psyche which in turn channels it into the body which cannot tolerate such intensity, and so it seeks release. Even though it feels extraordinarily good at the beginning, it eventually turns to pain from which one must escape. So love, in this sense, literally becomes too hot to handle.

In the romantic phase we feel the connection. We verbalize it as a heart or soul connection, but in essence it is an energy connection. Perhaps in a sense it is a soul connection because soul may not be a separate entity from flesh, but instead one end of an energy continuum where soul is the highest vibration and flesh the slowed down or frozen energy vibration.

As we entrain with another we activate vibrational energy throughout our being, from tissue to spirit.

So the interplay of energy seems to magnify its power, as it combines with, entrains with, and influences other energies, in an interconnected network of universal proportion. While perhaps the greatest influence is on systems in close proximity, there appear to be effects, nonetheless, on areas of the network far apart. And it appears that not only do like energies attract and tend to coalesce, but their blending produces *something more* than their combination. This brings to mind philosopher Ken Wilber's evolutionary mantra, "transcend and include."

So with all of this in mind, we can proceed with the "pair theory." To refer again to Robert Baker's *Joshua's Way,* Joshua, the pioneering philosopher/adventurer character in the book, has an experience in the desert facilitated by a sorcerer/shaman that enables him to see, finally, the endgame of his search for enlightenment, or the "journey to the source." As his vision becomes clear, at his moment of "full awakening," he sees an image of

millions of excited sperm swimming, racing powerfully to reach an awaiting egg which pulsates in anticipation. From the millions only hundreds grow near and fewer still arrive at the periphery of the egg, and then only one enters. The boundaries close and no more are admitted. Something new, different than either the sperm or the egg, is now born. How can either sperm or egg have any awareness of what they are to become? They can't. They can only do what they must do, and each gives up its own separateness and life to become part of something infinitely beyond either.

Superimposed upon these images are images of creatures emerging from the swamps and oceans to become land creatures. There can be no awareness of what existence would be like at that next level. These images are replaced by those of

Adam and Eve in the Garden of Eden; this is followed by images of the earth flooding and Noah gathering pairs of animals to put on the ark.

I begin to understand the message. *Nothing gets to the next level alone. It must be done in pairs.* In the allegory of paradise there are two, not one, and I and everyone else have been trying to get there alone, which is impossible.

Each must be part of a larger whole. Like the sperm and egg that sacrifice themselves, their separateness, and individual identity to produce a life force endlessly beyond themselves, so too must we do that at the spiritual level. The spirits must be joined, not temporarily as in a sexual experience or even longer such as when we are in love, but permanently so that each disappears into the greater whole produced by both. I realize that our first experience of being "in love" is the spirit's awakening to find another spirit with which to join. It is not just chemistry or physiology or the conscious finding of a partner but, instead, a directive from the life force that keeps pushing us to higher and higher levels of being. Because none of us have joined at that level we are all left with that deep-down feeling of a lack of completeness. We spend a lifetime searching for that level of connectedness, or delude ourselves into thinking we don't want or need or care about it. But we do.

There is no way to predict what the results and experiences of this joining would be. It would be the ultimate sacrifice, to be willing to give up one's existence as it is known for a greater life in an unknown dimension. In my mutual hypnosis experiments with Jeanne [Joshua's wife] we have sampled part of that dimension, perhaps one millionth of it.

I understand now what must be done. I have tried to enter into that domain keeping my separateness intact, and then bringing it back to this level of existence. What I am doing is analogous to trying to fit the ocean into a thimble, or a human into a sperm or egg.

It doesn't work that way.

The only way to that next dimension is to go to it with no expectation of returning. The butterfly, once a butterfly, can never again be a caterpillar. Is Jeanne willing to go there too?

This idea of two energies combining, joining to produce a new, greater (in an evolutionary "potential" sense) energy, is demonstrated time and again throughout history and literature. *Molecules of Emotion,* by Candace Pert, expands on and explains this idea from a "hard" scientific, chemical viewpoint but with a liberal injection of spirituality. In fact, Pert herself, a "Nobel quality" scientific pioneer, states unequivocally that her most inspired and innovative scientific discoveries were actually energies formed as a result of a separate energy joining with hers—resulting in a brand new, finer, more evolved energy.

Solo Displays of Spontaneous Excellence

But what of the seemingly *solo* displays of spontaneous excellence—zone experiences—that seem to pop out of nowhere, when individuals just burst forth with sudden, awe-inspiring performances? Is there collaboration in these instances? And if so, what, or who, is the source?

As we've seen, zone experiences are alignments, and specifically alignments of factors that produce optimum combinations of energies (remember that everything, ultimately, is energy in some form), resulting in highly efficient outputs of energy related to a specific *intention*. So when strong intention develops into clear focus, energies begin to mobilize and concentrate, and the clearer the focus—the stronger the intention—the greater the mobilization and concentration. The senses feed these energies specific, pertinent information to support the intention, and the chain of influence reaches the muscles, which are then equipped with a *coding*. Thus equipped, the coded muscles carry out the action in the most highly efficient way.

And so the source of these solo displays is the *already existing* energies within the organism, driven to alignment by intention, sensual input, and other influences, including *subtle energy*.

In the case of combined energies (from two people or more), the same process ensues but is "kicked' into action through sympathetic resonance. "Brainstorming sessions" are clear examples of this kind of action.

Future exploration will no doubt uncover how these energies, including the subtle energies, relate to endogenous substances (manufactured by the body) and will ultimately reveal the "formula" for zone entry. In other words, there could be a pill that elevates specific performance. This is the nature of the research that we do at the Holographic Golf Institute. We believe that we are on the brink of this and other transfomational discoveries. And if you have doubts as to whether science should introduce artificial means for things like elevating performance, rest easy, because you must remember that anything man creates, he creates from the very same substances of which he himself is made.

The brain, and the body, is a vast, incredibly complex network of informational exchange. And access to any and all information can be gained through *conscious intention,* or thought energy. The molecular, chemical correlates of this thought energy, called *neuropeptides,* "sniff out" and bind with the chemicals that direct the body to act, which then act in concert with the conscious intention. These neuropeptides find the appropriate (to the intention) receptors on the cell walls of the area involved (the area that directs the particular intended action), bind with them, and thus create a new energy (an action) out of the joining of thought energy (intention) with the body's informational (chemical) energy. It is simply a matter of using our own, innate energies. Mind does not direct body, and body does not direct mind. They are one and the same, just two parts of the same system: *bodymind.*

Consummation of the Marriage of Sense and Soul: Informed Focused Intention

As the twenty-first century begins, you can almost *feel* the world awakening. All over the globe, there are ever-expanding pockets of people talking about synchronicity, consciousness, and the coming together, finally, of science and religion, of fact and faith. This is what philosopher Ken Wilber calls the marriage of "sense and soul."

Candace Pert, in her book *Molecules of Emotion,* bridges the gap between hard science and spirituality, and shows that there is an underlying *chemical* basis for our emotions and the workings of the mind. The mind and body, therefore, are not separate, but one interconnected entity of energy, of substances arranged in unique configurations and combinations. This entity is called, more appropriately, *bodymind.* With Candace Pert's book, the stage is set for the marriage of sense and soul finally to be consummated.

The final piece of the puzzle is called *focused intention.* Through focused intention, the appropriate neuropeptides streak toward their receptors, carrying the specific informational "messages of intention" to the launch pad. As the receptors receive these messages, the informational substances then inform the appropriate cells of the body, which then moves in the most effective way, following the edict of the "information" it received.

Understanding this process explains why meditation and prayer, for so many centuries, have been considered such powerful practices. They both have, as their greatest common denominator, *conscious, or focused, intention.* And when the intention is *informed,* that is, when *knowledge* resides in the cellular makeup of the *bodymind,* the focused intention is laserlike in its clarity, and the action that follows is also pure.

Consider also that when the information contained in the organism is selected *appropriately* for a given intention, the power is increased. And the deeper and more complete the knowledge, the greater the power. Appropriate selection of specific information for a given intention is called instinct, or intuition. "Having a feeling" about something is a weak (or slow) connection (a low or slow-forming concentration of substances along the "pathway" of conscious thought relevant to the activity at hand) that nonetheless should be pursued. Most hunches prove to be accurate to some degree. And when you're "sure" of something, the concentration is strong. Conversely, when you have no clue as to how to proceed, intention is weak, and results are usually hit or miss.

CHAPTER 4

Evolution, Essence, Gurdjieff, and the Zone

As we've seen, operating in the zone is operating from *essence*, from our pure, untainted potential. Now let us understand that there is *evolution* and *involution*. To evolve means to become finer in substance, as our matter, and our being, becomes more *ordered* and we evolve ascendingly toward the Absolute. Involution means becoming more coarse, more dense, more *disordered*.

We humans, with our technological striving, have evolved technologically—we've evolved the things we use—but that is not so with *ourselves*. As a species, we've concentrated so much on the things around us that we've silently witnessed a *spiritual* involution, evidenced by the obvious signs of societal decay: high crime rates, apathy toward the young and the old, and the slow entropy of moral and religious values. Neglect of the children we casually produce and the irresponsible pillaging of our natural resources and the Earth itself complete the picture of general decay.

Even our technological advances, referred to by Edward O. Wilson as the "ratchet of progress," have brought us to the brink of disaster, and we must increasingly invent new technologies just to *survive*, let alone improve things. So here we are again. Recent archaeological finds suggest that perhaps we've been here before, many times. There is evidence that strongly suggests that mankind's development is an endless, repeating loop—a cycle. We evolve to a point, destroy ourselves, and start over. The big question now, overshadowing even the perennial existential question, is this: Is there a way out of the loop? Can we ever continue to evolve consciously—become finer and more ordered—and find our way to the mysteries we seek in our collective subconscious? With each technological evolvement along this endless loop, this question has undoubtedly been broached. But with each "conscious shock" the collective subconscious is deflected, so the circle—the loop—continues along an *ascending* octave. And each time this happens, we, as a species, intensify subconsciously our quest to answer the perennial question. Each epoch has its intellectual mutations—those evolutionary scouts who place their attention not on technological advance but on the potentiality of the human soul. They focus on the development of the only thing that really matters: the human essence.

It is this development—and only this development—that offers the hope of immortality. The human essence, not skyscrapers, computers, or spaceships, is eternal. Man's unique gift—he is the only animal capable of working on himself—has been appreciated and tended to by history's avatars. Gurdjieff summed it up in a way that can be heard by Everyman: "Your *only* aim can be to *not* perish like a dog."

This present epoch, reflecting the evolution of the collective subconscious—a fortunate mechanical *ascending* octave—has produced enough avatars to take us to the crossroads. We have the chance, especially with the symbolic new beginning of a new millennium, to break the loop and deflect the human trajectory upward, toward the finer, toward the Absolute, toward essence. When a work like *The Celestine Prophecy* can reach millions and millions, and theories like the holographic theory resonate with modern scientific minds, and when these ideas can filter their way even into various forms of *popular* human interest, then perhaps a critical mass is imminent. When a true critical mass is realized, the cycle, the loop, will be in jeopardy. The ratchet of progress will loosen, and further technological advance (necessary though it is) will always occur with primary consideration given to *man's* ascending inner evolution.

But to what altar do we pray? How do we attend to essence while searching the cosmos and the quantum field? How do we provide fuel and food for the increasing millions and at the same time ensure development of each individual soul? How can the scientists—the inventors, whose every moment is consumed with these technological tasks—tend to *themselves* and at the same time offer ways for the masses to awaken to their individual tasks?

There is no altar "around the corner," no "Temple of Answers." The clue has been with us from the earliest recorded "modern" histories, that is, the ones we've found. In *The Emerald Tablets,* medieval Egyptian prophet Hermes Trismegistus said, "As above, so below." And Pythagoras, Jesus, and all the others knew this and said it clearly enough. But the drumbeat and march of technological advance has always drowned it out with bigger buildings, more and "smarter" computers, and the whirring of engines—all supplemented by the constant drone of society's moans of anguish.

Gurdjieff, as well as others before him, saw the futility of the soapbox. They, and he, placed their bets on the appearance of increasing numbers of seekers—other avatar wannabes—who would *work* for the encoded message. The journey to the depths reveals truths only available at those depths, buried in the esoteric doctrine. Counting on increasing numbers of these potential teachers and bearers of the message "as above, so below," they left ample instruction. And now, with the crossroads of opportunity looming, the chance is finally here to transform the esoteric truths into common aim.

"The zone" is a catch-phrase of the times. And such a concept, possessing both universal scope and fundamental truth, is a perfect vehicle to board for the journey out of the loop and into an ascending evolutionary trajectory. Each of us can become finer. The payoff is in the immortality of the soul, a reward worth attention. It is the task of this teaching, and part of turning esoteric truths into a common aim, to outline a plan implementable by each individual, regardless of station. Let us begin by studying Gurdjieff's fundamental ideas, which, when grasped, can be linked to our present situation. Gurdjieff, somewhere, is smiling, knowing that at last his hope for transforming the "terror of the situation" is alive.

G. I. Gurdjieff

Georges Ivanovitch Gurdjieff was born in 1866 in the Greek quarter of Alexandropol in Russian Armenia. Gurdjieff spent over twenty years of his early life on a search for ancient wisdom. He found the earliest existing sources of all esoteric and exoteric teachings and, along with his fellow seekers, combined these wisdoms and doctrines into a coherent, integrated system.

Gurdjieff's system, known also as "The Fourth Way," has been called by many leading philosophical minds of the modern era the most complete cosmology ever put forth. It is a vast, complex teaching that answers all questions, especially the perennial existential one that was Gurdjieff's early call: "What is the significance of the life process on Earth of all the outward forms of breathing creatures and, in particular, what is the aim of human life?"

Gurdjieff's system is called his own because *he* assembled the pieces. And what makes it unique is that the "work"—"work on oneself"—is for life, in life. It is a practical way for every man to work on himself while still immersed in life, and to bring about his conscious spiritual development so that he evolves, becomes finer. He develops a soul, or "second body," which can gain immortality. This "work on oneself," available only to the animal man, can be the *only* true aim of existence. As Gurdjieff said, "Your *only* aim can be to *not* perish like a dog."

Gurdjieff is referred to with many titles: philosopher, master, spiritual teacher, saint, magician, hypnotist, and psychologist. But he referred to himself as simply a "teacher of dancing." What he meant, of course, was that he taught his pupils how to study, observe, and learn the intimate workings of their "machines." "As above, so below" tells us that if we study ourselves, which we conveniently inhabit, we study simultaneously the cosmos in its entirety. We search outer space and we search the quantum field. All we really have to do is search ourselves.

G. I. Gurdjieff died in 1949 and is buried in the family plot in Fontainbleu-Avon, near Paris.

Man's Centers, Man's Foods

Man is essentially an impersonal "machine," a wonderfully complex stimulus-response mechanism that "eats impressions and excretes behaviors." He is an apparatus characteristically devoid of self-cognizance and independent initiative, simply a cosmic transformer used by nature to separate the fine from the coarse and translate each to its proper sphere. In Gurdjieff's blueprint, the human machine burns simultaneously three foods of ascending refinement—food, air, and sensory impressions. These fuels blend to power five independent brains or "centers," which govern five functions: the intellectual center controls thinking; the emotional center our feelings; the moving center all learned external movement of the body in space; the instinctive center all the organism's unlearned internal functioning (respiratory, digestive, cardiovascular, etc.); and the sex center all authentic sexual manifestations.

The general design of this human machine or "food factory" is admirable, but in practice nothing works properly. The five centers—unsupervised and uncalibrated—relate inefficiently, jarring and grating on each other. Some subordinate parts have rusted, some are overheating, and others are inexplicably kept in mothballs. Breakdowns are frequent and replacement components difficult or impossible to obtain. Such a ramshackle contraption is neither efficient nor cost effective; after a short time it will certainly collapse.

Is the situation hopeless then—a closed Yezidi circle or an inescapable mechanistic prison? Sadly, it is, for the great masses of people who perversely imagine themselves already free. But it is not hopeless for everyone, fortunately—not for the statistically insignificant minority when frank and unbelievably painful confrontation of their interior slavery presages a long realistic struggle for emancipation.

Psychologists, take note: Gurdjieff is not propounding the ironclad determinism of Pavlov and Watson but a neobehaviorism that generously provides for the reentry of consciousness and free will. Man is a very special machine that, uniquely on Earth, can fully come to know and sense itself alive.

The three main centers, the moving, emotional, and intellectual, can signify type. Man #1 is rooted in the moving or physical center, man #2 the emotional center, and man #3 the intellectual center. These three ways are sometimes referred to as the way of the fakir, the way of the monk, and the way of the yogi.

Personality may mask but can never totally suppress these three categories' respective and lifelong inclinations toward the hand, the heart, and the head. Here are Shakespeare's Falstaff, Othello, Hamlet; Dostoevski's Dmitri, Alyosho, and Ivan. All human culture, all artistic forms, all religious and philosophical systems, may be classified and illuminated from this triadic standpoint. Where Gurdjieff's system differs from most psychologies is in stating that it is possible, through work on oneself, to "evolve type," through *conscious labor* and *intentional suffering.*

By working on all three centers simultaneously, "The Fourth Way," man can become man #4, *balanced* man, or even man #5, *unified* man. He can become finer, less coarse, less dense. He can broaden his dimension.

We will now discuss how the selective digestion of foods can evolve the machine, and more specifically, how each individual, irrespective of practical station in life or level of spiritual development, can work, while still immersed in "life," and can begin to develop his three main centers simultaneously. First, it is necessary to understand that men are born a certain, discernible "type." And remember, too, that through conscious "work on oneself," man has the capability to change his type. These types are basically, again, physical, emotional, and intellectual, and they are accompanied by postures and movements that are part of a definite and limited repertoire. A man spends his physical life going mechanically, unconsciously, from one "posture" to another, via the same automatic repetitive movements, movements that reflect his "type." Careful self-observation can reveal these patterns, and recognition of the repetitive patterns is the first step toward change.

Before getting into how our centers can be developed in an evolutionary way, we must look at the foods that "feed" and help refine them.

Man is a three-story factory. The first story houses the moving center; the middle story, the emotional center; and the upper story, the intellectual center. It should be noted, however, that each story, in turn, has its own stories, with parts of each center in each main center.

The foods that feed these centers are (1) the ordinary foods that we eat and the water we drink, (2) the air that we breathe, and (3) the impressions that we take in through our senses. Our physical bodies, mostly responsible for our physical movements, rely on the first kind of food—ordinary food and water. And this food, regardless of its *earthly* diversity, remains generally the same. The same is true of the air we breathe. While the quality and pureness of the first two kinds of foods can perhaps be optimized, they remain within a limited and definite realm. But the third kind of food, that of impressions, can be converted by us, consciously and willfully, to whatever quality we decide. So their "digestion" can be directed consciously. And here's a big signpost on our journey: we eat impressions and excrete behavior. The impressions that we digest become the behaviors that we exhibit. And the impressions that we digest can be fed to our centers intentionally with a quality that we are capable of determining. In other words, we can *transmute* impressions.

Now let us go back to types, movements, and postures. We said that man is capable of willfully changing his type. This can only be done when man changes his being. And to change his being, he must work on his centers and develop them in a balanced, harmonious way. As a man begins to observe his movements and postures, he begins, with work, to change them. And as his postures and movements change, his being and his type can change. In Gurdjieff's system, this was only possible through a certain exercise, and he called it the "stop" exercise. Here's how the "stop" exercise works.

The teacher, quite randomly, will give the verbal command, "Stop!" The student, immediately upon receiving the signal, must freeze completely. The physical position is held, no matter how uncomfortable. The facial expression is held just as it was at the time of the command. The gaze is held in exactly the same position, and the degree of tension in the muscles is held exact. If the student becomes unable to support himself and begins to fall, he must do so without trying to break the fall. He must fall like a "sack" to the ground. The student, by repeated experiences of this "stop" exercise, will come to observe himself, his postures, his movements. He will also become aware of postures and movements that he usually never notices because of their "automatic" nature. This "stop" exercise, used as a tool for self-observation, for "remembering" oneself, is a fundamental building block in Gurdjieff's system, for without self-knowledge, without knowing how our "machine" works, change is not possible.

This "self-remembering," which sharpens one's attention, is a bridge to self-knowledge. And it is this sharpening of attention that ultimately can lead to conscious control of the way in which the "foods of impressions" are assimilated.

And, quite simply, if we "eat" certain impressions, we will "excrete" certain behaviors. *The zone, which is behavior of a refined nature,* is only exhibited when a certain combination of foods is assimilated. This is why, when functioning in our normal "waking" state of consciousness, which is in reality a state of "waking sleep"—the subconscious being the optimum state—those particular combinations of foods are blended accidentally and only rarely, and why the "zone," as it is called—that tear in the fabric of so-called reality—appears so mysteriously and elusively. To inch closer to intentional, willful displays of our higher potentials, we must inch closer to intentional, willful combinations of the various foods that nourish and develop our three main centers. It is, then, full, harmonious, and equal participation of these centers that contributes to the phenomena we call "zone experiences."

We'd now like to give you an example of how such progressions of actions take place. First you decide that you want to do something. You have the desire, the feeling to do it. If it is a strong feeling, it may compel you to take action. Your emotional center, which "gets the vibes going," is fully involved, with its energy focused on the desired action. Intellectually, mentally, you draw on the knowledge of how this particular desired action must proceed. You *think* about *how* to do it. What's left, of course, is for the physical center to carry out the desires and plans of the other two centers. As you can well see, without the *desire,* or without the *knowledge,* the act itself has little chance for full efficiency.

Highly successful action must include participation of all three centers. The physical center performs its action with efficiency proportionate to the input from the intellectual center and the emotional, or feeling, center. How does this work? To answer, let's look at some recent findings from the cutting edge of research in quantum mechanics.

Sympathetic Resonance

When a guitar string is plucked, the strings nearest to it tend to vibrate toward the same frequency as the *driven* frequency. This same phenomenon, called sympathetic resonance, is applicable to all matter in our world, visible in (to our limited sense awareness) greatly varying degrees. It is why grandfather

clocks in great numbers in the same room will tend to synchronize as time passes, all eventually "swinging" together. It is
why "birds of a feather flock together," people fall in love, and
teams "catch fire" and work in unison in the midst of frenzied
action. A driven frequency of vibration influences the vibrations of nearby (a relative term) matter. It is why a charismatic
person draws you into his sphere and you "resonate" with him
because his vibration is "strong" and influential.

Man, being "three brained," or a three-centered being, produces vibrations of potential dominance in three ways—emotionally, intellectually, and physically. In keeping with this idea
of sympathetic resonance, it is not surprising to note that to
increase the likelihood of a physical action, the *thought* and *feelings* regarding the desired action should act as the driven frequency to which the ensuing frequencies should resonate. In
other words, by keeping the *thoughts* of an action and the *desire*
for said action *uppermost* in one's consciousness, those mental
and emotional vibrations become the dominant ones in the
field of the organism, and the vibrations of the physical movement will tend to approximate them.

This is the underlying principle of physics for common
human psychological acts such as the "assumptive close" in
sales, the "suggestibility" of advertising, or "brainwashing tac-
tics." It is also the sometimes honorable strategy for political,
religious, and motivational influence. Very simply, it is the
power of sympathetic resonance at work, and this power can,
with practice and knowledge, be developed and directed to a
great degree.

When discussing resonance, it is important to remember
that an energy source, when in proximity to other like forms,
is either dominant or subordinate. Its influence can be positive
and energizing or negative and debilitating. Use of energy,
therefore, is directed by intent.

This is one reason why an important aspect of Gurdjieff's
system included not displaying negative emotions. A form's
negative vibrations literally suck energy from other forms in

proximity to it in proportion to the distance separating them. Forms of a different density, which are less affected, serve as conduits between them.

"Zone" experiences are expressions, in action, of man's three main centers ridding themselves of accumulations of fine substances (energies) that have crystallized through either chance or intention. It's like the laugh releasing excess joy. If you were to carefully chart your peak, or zone, experiences, you would begin to see, over time, a cyclical pattern. This cyclical pattern, when not perceived, seems random. Everything in our universe is cyclical by nature, and will actualize by nature, but man, possessing the potential for free will and conscious action, can control to some degree these normal cycles. And man is the only animal that can do this. So man's ability to "work on himself," and in particular his ability to work on his three main centers simultaneously, can enable him to call his own shots—to some degree—to arrange his energies in particular ways that are to his benefit. Let's take a closer look at just how man can work on, and refine the energies of, his three main centers.

To work on his moving or physical center, a man must first have knowledge of, by studying closely, his *machine*. Studying postures and movements can provide this knowledge, which can be used to make his machine work efficiently. And since the machine actually performs action, it should operate at high efficiency, conserve and store its available energy, and assume postures and movements conducive to and appropriate for the desired action. This machine should be provided with fuel in sufficient quantities and of appropriate content, and this applies to ordinary food #1, which is food, food #2, air, and food #3, impressions, which, through sympathetic resonance, can affect the substances of the machine in positive ways.

In addition, this machine should be exercised regularly in order to keep its working parts in good order, and kept clean, to maximize its vitality and reduce susceptibility to harmful outside influences (such as disease). Careful self-observation and honest assessment can reveal which combinations of ordinary food best fuel each machine—for they vary in requirements—but the machine is inherently efficient at separating the coarse from the fine. And the same goes for air, the medium in which our machines live. It is best to attempt to subject the machine to "clean air." But again, this process of separating is automatic, and it cannot be controlled. But the third type of food, the food of the sensory impressions that we take in, while also subject to automatic assimilation if unfiltered, can uniquely be filtered and then translated to the physical center as energies, or food, of a refined nature, resulting in action influenced by them.

Owing to our technological advance—the ratchet of progress—we have become subject to a wide variety of outside influences. These influences can deflect our natural assimilation of impressions. To give an example, hundreds of years before our "technological advance," an accidental deterrent to a man's intentions, such as a bird's call scaring away a man's prey, would be objectively dealt with, not at all deflecting his intended action, which he would immediately resume without a second thought. Modern man, however, on a trip to the grocery in his car, when "cut off" by a discourteous driver, could be upset by the incident to the point of "forgetting" his mission and thus failing to "bring home the milk." The way that he deals with the impression, random events beyond his control, determines whether or not the trajectory of his energies proceeds as intended, or deflects and degenerates into something less.

This simple example reveals that through our conscious will we have the power to filter the impression into something fine or coarse, and that this process can affect the next step in our actions. It is the practice of self-observation, self-remembering, and objective reasoning that enables us to break free of the automatic responses to which we are accustomed, or, rather, enslaved.

Now let's shift our attention to another cause of our automatism, namely, the masking of our essence. *Essence* is what we are at birth, and essence is determined by heredity, geographical locale, planetary influence, and combinations of many other complex and unknown factors. *Personality,* however, is what we develop from environmental and circumstantial influence, and from the type of impressions received and how they are assimilated. With the appearance of the ego, the young child begins to develop personalities, or manifestations, for each circumstance and for interacting with each other person. These "masks," or personalities, are really buffers that protect, reinforce, or deflect, depending on the needs of essence.

The fragile new ego needs the buffers to build its self-image, and the formation of these masks, these personalities, becomes an endless loop. The "reel of personalities" gets larger and larger, unless through "work on oneself" the reel can be unwound and essence rediscovered. It is this "return to essence" that is the goal of self-work. Only then can a man live in total honesty and make efficient use of his energies.

So how does man—"the lying animal," as Gurdjieff calls him, the only animal capable of lying, and yet, on the other hand, the only animal capable of "working on itself"—make the most of his energies? First it is necessary to understand that a man is given, each day, a certain amount of available energy. When this supply becomes depleted, it must be reacquired through rest and/or nourishment and stored again. According to Gurdjieff, next to each center, and here we include the instinctive center, are two small accumulators that supply energy to the center. These are all connected together and, in turn, are connected to one large accumulator. These "supply houses" are constantly emptying and refilling and can, on occasion, become depleted to the point where the large accumulator becomes used and drained, requiring conservation, and rest and nourishment for replenishment. If the large accumulator itself were ever completely depleted of its reserves, the organism would die. But this is rare. Before this could happen, the person would faint and go on "automatic pilot" until rejuvenated.

There are two interesting human acts that have a lot to do with the "give and take" of energy. These are the acts of *yawning* and *laughing*. Yawning replenishes energy. It draws from the accumulator and is an instinctive action, though it can also be a very valuable conscious technique. Watch footage of big cats as they prepare to pounce on their prey. They yawn as they summon the energy required for the upcoming "burst." Mountain climbers, as they ascend steep grades and become fatigued, will yawn repeatedly in attempts to draw upon these reserves.

The act of laughing, however, is the release of superfluous energy, energy that goes unused and "overflows." If a man uses his energy efficiently and judiciously, he has no leftover, unused energy and so no need to laugh. It is said that Jesus Christ never laughed, and there are no existing writings or teachings, including the Gospels, that make any mention of him laughing. But in Jesus Christ we're speaking of perhaps a unique—in degree of actualization—and highly developed being. For ordinary man, it's not an easy thing to regulate and economize our daily allotments of energy. There are many potential drains on our individual and collective supplies, and one must be in a constant state of self-remembering—awareness—in order to avoid being sapped dry.

The zone experience occurs during a state of high and focused energy, and that supply, for that duration, remains focused and adequate in quantity. Any influences, internal or outside, mental or physical, can weaken our energy supply. And when the "fuel line" is clogged, or shut down, or even polluted, then the machine's operation is immediately affected. This is why the zone experience can be so fleeting and elusive. It is a fragile thing unless we have objective, conscious knowledge of the way it works.

As an example, a person could be playing tennis and going along in a flow of efficiency of rare quality, playing his "best ever," when suddenly he thinks of something derogatory that his co-worker said to him a week ago. Or over on another court, a young girl, playing with her friends, lets out a loud shriek after an errant shot. In either case—zap!—his energy is diverted, first, mentally; then second, unless he can fill this interval with a "recovery technique," emotionally; and, finally, if the "outside shock" is allowed free rein, physically. And the zone experience is over.

Here we have reached a critical juncture—intervals that, depending on how they're filled, can lead to a continuation of the trajectory (of great performance) or a deflection of it. At this point, "sleeping man," man who doesn't work on himself, is at the mercy of mechanical processes, and his experience falls apart as his energy becomes diluted and corrupted. But "conscious man," a man who is awake, who works on himself, and who has objective knowledge and uses objective reason, knows how to deal with this interval appropriately—indeed, as a fundamental requirement, is *aware* of the interval.

Recognizing an interval depends on a man's awareness—that is, he must *remember himself* and not get carried away unconsciously by mechanized processes. When the tennis player hears the shriek and dwells on its potential consequences (outside negative shock), or remembers the negative comments and experiences negative emotion (internal negative shock), he will, if not conscious and "awake," lose the moment. If, however, the man simply "witnesses" the occurrence and uses a reinforcing technique, he will go on unaffected. The reinforcing techniques may be certain breathing exercises, visualizations, postures or movements that "kick him back" (into his previous rhythm), or various other techniques, which are discussed in detail in other sections of this book, that are conducive to, and indeed a necessary part of, the zone experience.

All of the previous discussion was about how a zone experience can be prolonged and interruption of it diverted. But what about how to *get into* that elusive state? What steps can be taken to get it started? How can a performance get off to an extraordinary start? This question is perhaps the most important, because the answers have wide-ranging implications, from early stage development of the individual all the way up to influences on a global societal scale. The actualizing of potential and starting and maintaining evolutionary trajectory are one and the same. To begin with, one must have an aim. And the primary aim should be to "work on oneself," to evolve energetically, to separate the coarse (for example, negative emotion) from the fine (for example, the joy of helping another). With this always and in everything uppermost in one's mind, any action will be evolutionary. The aim will permeate all action, all planning.

Having this primary "building block" in place is the beginning "do" of do-re-mi, the "process of octaves." As the action progresses, regardless of the worldly nature of the goal, having this primary aim acts as the "driven frequency," from whose positive influence proximate frequencies will benefit. And when the intervals occur, the missing semitones between mi-fa and ti-do, the frequency of the primary aim will increase the possibility of finding the appropriate, positive shock necessary for continuation of the evolutionary action toward its goal. But it is important to remember that the only ongoing, permanent aim is continuous "work on oneself," development of one's *being*, throughout one's life. Then it is possible, Gurdjieff says, to achieve, by literally transforming the matter of one's whole being into something finer, a crystallization of the soul, through which one can achieve immortality and not "perish like a dog."

In order for you, as an individual, to utilize this knowledge, a process is needed. This process must be practical and appropriate to your "life" situation, for it is vital, and one of this system's main tenets, to "work on oneself" *in* life, not withdraw from it. This process serves as a guide and enables you to take the necessary and appropriate steps to work on yourself regardless of the environment or circumstance. In fact, as you will see, some of your most meaningful self-work can come in the midst of chaos or times of personal turbulence.

The process begins for everyone with this cornerstone: the

consistent practice of self-remembering, as often as possible, by any means available. Initially, artificial reminders, such as hourly "chime" alarms or some such prompt, are useful and indeed necessary. Eventually, one should strive to get to the point of self-remembering without outside reminders.

The next step is in the reception of sensory impressions. Due to heightened awareness of sensory input as a result of self-observation, the impressions that we "take in" through our senses are "fed" to our centers, but it is this "conscious reception," as opposed to a mechanical absorption, that makes it possible for the "energy" of these impressions to be distributed accurately and appropriately. This "selective assimilation" serves to efficiently nourish the centers, allowing for their better functioning in a *conscious* way. When an impression is received by the senses, and remains at the mercy of mechanical (unconscious) processes, then the center most absorbed in the activity of the moment will process the impression first. This is, as you can see, a random process, leaving any possibility of efficient functioning strictly to chance. For instance, if the moving center is immersed in an activity that requires its full participation, then an impression picked up by a sense that is normally attached to another center may inappropriately involve that center in the activity of the moment, thereby diluting the moving center's participation and lowering performance.

The next step in the process involves determining the relevance of sensory input to the activity at hand. To do this, it is necessary, first of all, to categorize sensory input. As we receive information, we must at the same time be aware of which center is *most* involved in the action of the moment. We must then identify which center this new input would best serve. If we decide that this input would not assist the "working" center, then it must be immediately discarded and ignored, and we must go right back to the activity at hand. This should be done as quickly as possible so as not to "lose the flow" of our actions. With practice this process can be completed without a "break in the rhythm." If the new input, however, would assist the working center, then it should be "added to the mix," and this is done by going right back to the activity, with this new input kept uppermost in the mind. This will serve to "blend it in," and contribute to the evolution of our actions toward our goal.

Most of our actions fall short of their intended target simply because we allow sensory input to dilute our attention. When the intellectual center, for instance, becomes inappropriately involved with activity of the moving center, we tend to overanalyze, or "train away our natural gifts." Instead of relying on our instincts and knowledge gained through experience, the intellectual center's untimely involvement results in a mechanized overanalysis, and our natural instincts are stifled.

Sometimes the pitfalls can be subtle. Witness the golfer who, cruising along in a good rhythm, playing well effortlessly, suddenly overhears his playing companions discussing the correct positioning of the hands on the club—grip theory. The golfer then remembers his own struggles with learning the correct grip, and inexplicably looks down at his own grip and begins checking it out, moving it around, wondering if it's "exactly right." All of a sudden, he's questioning the "correctness" of his own grip and starts thinking about it. And then something about it just doesn't feel quite right—just like that. He is out of the zone, and out of rhythm. His ensuing "slump" might last for days, weeks, maybe months. This episode might even lead him to question the correctness of all of his fundamentals and cause him to seek to change and "improve" his technique. This scenario happens all the time, even occasionally to world-class players.

When I used to teach golf full time, I was constantly reminding students that (especially for better players) poor shots are most often *mistakes* and not fundamental flaws in their techniques. If they had a serious fundamental flaw, they would never be able to play all of the fine shots that they do on a consistent basis. A poor shot is not necessarily a reason to question one's technique. Instead, try to see where and why the mistake was made, and go on to the next shot, changing nothing. If a longtime pattern of poor shots develops, and frequency increases, then a longer look at mechanics is warranted.

The functioning of the centers relevant to the "zone experience" can be summed up in this way: The center primarily involved in an activity should only receive information from other centers that is helpful and relevant. This is the only way that the zone experience can be sustained, because this process is one of an *ascending* evolutionary nature. It negates the effects of the natural, inevitable entropic influences that constantly "bombard" the process from "outside," any of which, if not deflected, can stop the momentum of any action. So a blueprint, a plan, for promoting states of high functioning—for entering the zone—might look something like this:

Through the practice of self-observation we can "peel away" layers of personality and find our essence. When we operate from essence, we operate with all centers in unison, undisturbed by outside influences whose entrée was "personality." When the centers work harmoniously, each informing the others with positive influence, then this state of high efficiency—of focused attention and *informed* instinct—the zone—can be reached.

Universal Law

Gurdjieff interpreted and applied a set of Universal Laws. The Law of Sameness, as put forth by Hermes M. Trismegistus in *The Emerald Tablets,* qualifies to be included. This Law of Sameness, or "as above, so below"as Trismegistus put it, is another way of saying that all matter is composed of a combination of certain substances in varying quantities and forms, an endless set of potential combinations that manifests in an infinite number of frequencies, densities, and shapes.

The significance of this law is that it is possible for us to study the universe in "our own backyards," that is, we can study *ourselves,* and in doing so unlock the mysteries of the cosmos.

The real mystery lies in the infinite nature of the world we experience.

The harder scientists try to pin down the facts and formulas and map out the way things are, the wider the vista broadens and expands before their very eyes. Science and faith have long been on a collision course, and the crash will result in a blending of each into the other. *As above, so below* is the *only* formula with any staying power—the only set scientific doctrine. And based on ancient knowledge handed down in esoteric circles by the Masters of Wisdom (see John G. Bennett's book, *Masters of Wisdom: An Esoteric History of the Spiritual Unfolding of Life on This Planet*), there is another Universal Law, the Law of Orbit.

Everything, it seems, is orbiting other things and, at the same time, is itself also being orbited. The smallest particles we've found in quantum physics, as well as the largest objects observed by telescopes, are all spinning around, oscillating, orbiting, and *humming*. George Leonard, in his profound and eloquent book *The Silent Pulse,* says that what lies at the heart of these vibrations is a silent *pulsing.* Sound has long been thought to have been the original emanation, and the resultant reality simply the continuing echo of the primordial sound, branching out, like a tree or the endless octaves of the musical scale, into an ever-increasing array of energy of infinite variation. But at the source, at the heart, of each manifestation lies the original sound. And that is the goal of our search, both outward and inward.

As the echoes of the primordial sound branch out as fields of energy, mixing in random proportion and manifesting in infinite forms, the densities of masses create "pulls" of varying degree on other forms of energy—other matter. Ultimately, the pull results in the establishment of an orbit, or circling, of the dominant mass. This "dominance" does not mean "better"—just stronger in terms of density, mass, and "pulling power." Keeping in mind always and in everything the universal mantra of "as above, so below," we can examine our lives—our reality—in these terms.

Perhaps man's fascination with music has to do with the desire for the familiar womblike security of the primordial sound. With each "new" piece of music, or combination of sound energies, we perhaps draw closer to experiencing the original emanation, the primordial sound—the driven frequency. It could be that man's infinite quest is a *search for sound*. And it could be that the first sounds that we hear help to set our personal orbit, and that it is shaped constantly by all future sounds.

Sounds, the limitless combinations of energies, literally resonate with and drive the frequencies that make up our very being. They can direct us, they can deteriorate us, and they can resonate with us. The Universal Law of "Three" is at work: positive, negative, and neutralizing.

Whose energy is not uplifted by the happy voices of loved ones, or terribly and instantly depleted by the sound of their heartbroken cries? Music, as we've already discussed, has the same effects, if it is *objective* music (see appendix 1), and the same with the visual arts. And the energies of the sounds of nature hold the same power over our own energies. They can evoke emotion.

To relate to the power of music over the emotions, imagine watching a sad movie without the mournful, wailing soundtrack. It bears no resemblance to, and has a fraction of the effect of, watching the same movie with the music. The sounds touch our souls and stimulate, for better or worse, our hearts.

The power and magnetic draw of chanting monks can be attributed to the approximation of the primordial sound. These chants are basic tones, not venturing out into distant octaves, and their powerful, repetitive vibrations touch our essence.

If we could devise and apply just the right stylus, we could replay the sounds of the ancient past, on cave and canyon walls, sidewalks, and walls of houses. Every sound, every word ever spoken, is recorded forever in the universe, ready to be discovered when the perfect stylus comes along.

When two people are strongly attracted to one another, sexually, emotionally, or intellectually, it's because their frequencies match up very well, very closely. And likewise, instant dislike, or a "personality clash," is an example of frequencies that are widely different in range. Simply put, some people resonate with other certain people, and some people don't resonate with other certain people at all.

When stars collide, when the pulling power of two people draw them together, newer, finer energies are created. Examine your orbit to see whom you circle, and who circles you. Which people do you spend the most time with or "run into" on a regular basis? Widen the circles around yourself, the "star," and then see who orbits you and whom you orbit, who your pulling star is. Whom are you now magnetically drawn to, and who is drawn to you? The answers are valuable, for they tell a lot about who and what you are and what kind of energy you have. The answers can provide "information for transformation."

The Role of Objective Art: Music, Symbols, and Sacred Dance

There are two kinds of art, *subjective* and *objective*. Subjective art is subject to interpretation, with response depending on association, while objective art has specific, predictable, even intentional effects on *everyone* who encounters it. Many ancient "works of art"—certain sculptures, statues, monuments, etc.—were not created for aesthetic value, though some have that additional quality. They were constructed or created for a purpose, for their specific effects on the people who viewed them. These effects included various emotions, such as feelings of loyalty, and could provoke predictable actions among large groups of people. These and other forms of symbols make up one facet of what we call objective art.

Other facets of objective art are made up of music created to be objective, and what is called sacred dance, which includes movements and postures that speak a certain language. It is a language that can be understood by the feelings, and the feelings (and feeling center) can be influenced to bring about contributions from other centers to further the aim of the feelings that have been stirred to initiate action.

In ancient times, and even today in hidden cultures, the language of dance and movement was and is an important part of human life, with various certain postures and movements influencing desired actions, such as hunting, fighting, reproducing, or nurturing and healing. Since man's beginnings, certain movements and postures have been associated with certain specific actions, and centuries of the evolutionary process have rendered these as genetic traits, as instinct. But again, through diligent self-observation, a man can become acquainted with his "machine" and then intentionally begin to adopt a whole new set of postures and movements, *consciously,* and thus change his actions. He can train his machine to function not as an automaton, but as a servant to his will. Only then, as Gurdjieff says, can a man be a *real* man. Only then, he says, can a man really "do" anything, and not just *automatically* react to impressions and environmental circumstances in a programmed manner. These concepts of self-transformation, all rooted in the science of self-observation, can be applied to any human endeavor and that is the point of this whole book—that the zone is applicable to any activity, and that it can be cultivated and encouraged by anyone, at any time.

Before delving more deeply into the vital role of music (sound), let's take a look at symbols, their origins, and their meanings. Symbols, such as the cross, are constructs that tell wordless stories, evoke stories of words, and portray laws. One symbol in particular, the enneagram, exhibits the fundamental Universal Laws, the *Law of Three* and the *Law of Seven.* Briefly, the Law of Three, applicable to all phenomena in our universe, states that everything is the result of three forces: an active force, a passive force, and a neutralizing force. Another way of stating this is that *the upper blends with the lower to actualize the middle.* In evolutionary terms, it would be stated that as something (any-thing) *evolves*, it *transcends and includes* what existed previously.

The Law of Seven, also called "the law of octaves," states that all events proceed through octaves, either ascending or descending through steps of vibratory frequencies. Based on the musical scale, which incidentally was an ancient invention that was lost and then discovered again, this law also states that within these steps are two missing half-tones, between mi-fa and ti-do, and that events, as they proceed, are subject to a change in trajectory at these stages. So outside forces, or "shocks," deflect all development, or, if appropriately orches-trated, these shocks can "stay the course" of a particular event.

The enneagram, which is a circle divided into nine equal parts, contains all the knowledge of the universe. The origin of this secret symbol is virtually untraceable due to its age, but it is a universal hieroglyph complete in its universal law. Gurdji-eff hinted that it may date back to the Sarman brotherhood, or perhaps the Essenes, the formation of which predated by two centuries the time of Christ, when secret schools of knowledge were taught and belonged to by the "masters of wisdom." The Essene brotherhood was formed by the esoteric circle or caste of the Magi in Judea. Jesus Christ received his early training and initiation from the Essene brotherhood.

At any rate, study of the universal symbol of the enneagram is an important matter, and one that we will be discussing at length. But the importance of symbols in tracing our origins and discovering the workings of our universe cannot be over-stated. I encourage you to learn about and study the ennea-gram, for it can be revelatory in many ways and can be used as a valuable tool as one works toward the alchemy of self-trans-formation. I recommend P. D. Ouspensky's *In Search of the Miraculous: Fragments of an Unknown Teaching* for further and more in-depth discussion of the enneagram, and then J. G. Bennett's *Enneagram Studies*.

Now we come to the power of sound to transform, more

specifically, music—that creative (and potentially objective) formation of sound. Dating back to the origins of music, its primitive form was nonetheless based on rhythm and man's perception of patterned combinations of sound. There were chants and primitive forms of drumming or rhythmic "tapping," and these patterned sounds, it was quickly discovered, could elicit certain actions, as a result of certain *feelings* or *thoughts.* Even "smoke signals," an early form of language, could be called wordless and soundless "music," as they were based on patterns emerging in a certain "rhythm." Poetry, it might be said, is the bridge between language and music. But music (or language) of this sort is still subjective—subject to interpretation based on association. You might, for example, hear an upbeat, joyous tune on the saddest day of your life, and that "happy" song will forever, for you, be associated with and evoke feelings of sadness. But objective music is based on universal law and can be constructed (through intentional alignment of sounds) to evoke predictable, certain responses in all people, all the time. It is said, for instance, that music could be composed that would freeze water, or kill a man instantly. Perhaps in the practical world, this theoretical possibility remains remote, but in lesser form it is certainly within our reach and of great value. Let us explain.

With objective analysis, it can be found that for each individual different impressions (including especially certain music), due to associations or simply due to *physical response* to certain sounds or combinations of sounds, evoke predictable action consistently. In Michael Murphy's book with Rhea White, *The Psychic Side of Sports,* many famous examples of this are cited, including the great amateur golfer Bobby Jones, who said that, while playing his best, certain melodies were being heard in his "inner ear" as he swung the club, and sometimes he would even deliberately hum his favorite tunes, and then "time" his swing to them. To hear your national anthem, for example, or your high-school fight song evokes pride and the willingness to defend.

What we propose here, in order for you to take advantage of this powerful tool—the tool of sound—is to start taking a careful inventory of sounds and your response (thoughts first, feelings second, actions third) to them. Over time, this personal "collection" of yours will reveal definite patterns. Once you have established an extensive, pattern-filled inventory, you can begin to experiment by subjecting yourself to certain sounds (e.g., music) *prior* to an event.

For instance, if a certain song *always* results in feelings of compassion, understanding, and patience, then play that song on your earphones before that meeting that has the potential for being heated and adversarial. Or if a certain song makes you feel relaxed and optimistic, play it before a personal performance—whatever that might be—where those attributes are a plus. If you are by nature a shy or meek person, and some song (perhaps a march or anthem) stirs feelings of exuberance or assertiveness, then listen to it before an important negotiation where it is vital that you not get "run over." And for your health, play sounds that *make you happy.*

Feelings elicited by these types of stimuli are always accompanied by beneficial chemical release. It was once said by an esteemed psychiatrist that music or "wild dancing" has the potential to "empty entire wings of mental hospitals." But go into most nursing homes, asylums, or hospitals, and you'll find virtually no trace of stimuli designed to uplift or "heal" individuals on a *personal* level. Quite the contrary: you'll more often find darkened halls and rooms, music (if any) of an inappropriate nature, and little *personal design of direct stimuli.* And it is this—the *intentionally planned design of personal stimuli,* along with the *ability to transmute the food (or energy) of impressions*—that can combine to propel us toward enhanced performance.

Let's look more closely at planned design of stimuli. Along with music, other influences can be the art with which we surround ourselves, and this definition of "art" is broad in scope—taking in even our furniture and things like the colors around us. There have actually been studies made on the effects of the colors of the clothes we wear, with results that suggest a definite, almost universal effect. So, in effect, though the ability to compose music that would freeze water may remain elusively esoteric, milder yet still effective forms of objective art can be used to produce predictable and desirable results. This use of objective art, that is, to influence, is a secret long employed by advertisers. Michael Murphy touches on this in *Golf in the Kingdom,* and he mentions the connection to the "occult" or to "magic." In an alchemy where the zone takes the place of gold, the "lead" of average performance is transformed.

It is important to remember that just as music and other art forms can have positive transformational effects, inappropriate use or exposure can have the opposite effect. The idea of moving toward the zone is one of an *ascending* nature, or octave, while normal performance that degenerates is of a descending nature. And the impressions we receive, and the effect they have on our centers, determine the course of an event. While it may not be possible always to orchestrate a favorable environment for our activities, it is very possible to control what we *do* with the elements of that environment. By being conscious, we can feed off the positives and transform the negatives. At all times, *stay conscious, stay open* to your environment. It contains all the secrets to your personal alchemy available to you at every moment.

The Enneagram

Now we come to the part of this book where you will be provided with a tool that you can use at any time, anywhere, to instantly give you two things: (1) a picture of where you are at any present moment, and (2) a blueprint for getting closer to your goal and for elevating the effectiveness of your future actions. Basically, the enneagram is a circle that contains two figures, a hexad and a triad, and that represent the endless cyclical loop of everything, as well as zero. The two figures form nine points that touch the circle. The triad, at points 9, 3, and 6, represents the Law of Three—or the law of three forces—and the hexad, at points 1, 4, 2, 8, 5, and 7 (following the flow of movement between those six points), represents the Law of Seven, or the law of octaves. The movement of time and action flow is represented by the direction of the arrows. The progression 1-4-2-8-5-7 is a perpetually repeating one obtained when 1 is divided by 7 (1 divided by 7 = .142857142857, etc.). When 1 is divided by 3, another repeating progression (in this case, .33333 . . .) is obtained. When one-third is added, we get .66666 . . ., and another third produces .99999 . . . (giving us the 9-3-6 points of the triad). Hence the symbolic connection to the two universal laws of perpetuity and creative action. With the enneagram any process can be seen in such a way to show us where the weaknesses are, and what is needed to "keep the cycle going" around the perpetuating circle and infinitely ascending octaves.

Any process can be examined in its entirety, so the critical areas or junctures are exposed to an overview, a grand view, and a microview. Your own experience with exploring and studying the enneagram will constantly result in your own insights and your own ideas and applications. But relevant to what we're studying—namely, the zone—there are several interesting observations that appear to be the keys to unlock the mystery—the seemingly random appearance of the zone.

First of all, according to the Law of Seven, there are two places in an octave where "conscious shocks" from outside are needed in order for the process to be completed. Without these shocks, or influences, the process is subject to deviation. Now, again according to the universal Law of Seven, every process has a point of no return, or irrevocability, at which point recovery from deviation is not possible. To borrow an example from J. G. Bennett's chapter titled "Kitchen at Work," in serving a meal, if the kitchen helper lays out the wrong utensils, all is not lost. The staff can recover and go on, and the process will go on undeterred. But if the chef burns the food, that particular process—serving that meal—is stopped irrevocably. And this principle can be applied to any process.

So the first step in planning an event (or performance) is determining the first interval—the point of no return—and also determining what will fill the interval—what "shock" from outside can be consciously provided. An example of this could be a "warning" of some sort, before the process begins, of where and when to provide this "outside action." This becomes easier, of course, in a repeated process, where one is intimately familiar with the steps involved.

The second step, and perhaps the most important for sustaining the evolutionary aspect of the performance, which, as always, means to *transcend* and *include*, is filling the second interval appropriately. The second interval, between ti-do, is actually full completion. It is not just *finishing*, for there is a vast and profoundly influential difference between finishing something and *completing* something. *Completion* must fill the second interval, for only then is a *bridge* completed between octaves— a bridge that must exist in order for the trajectory to continue. It is one thing to experience moments of elevated performance, but it is quite another to sustain it.

Let us give you a practical example of "finishing" versus "completing." A golfer is on a roll, in the "zone," and plays a great shot to the sixteenth green, the ball heading straight to the flag. In his excitement, he turns to his playing partners, beaming, and says something like, "That's going to be close. I can't hit it any better," and doesn't even watch the ball bounce on the green and roll toward the hole. In his premature excitement he fails to watch the shot to completion—until the ball comes to rest—and thereby interrupts the flow of sensual feedback of the total shot. This failure to complete the process, this interruption in the flow, could very well break the rhythm down, dilute the quality, and this subtle break could adversely affect the next attempt by virtue of interrupting the trajectory of what was happening. This break, in effect, subjects the next attempt to the uncertainty of "starting again," from the beginning of a whole new octave of a "new" process, which lacks the ascending momentum of what was happening before the "break" occurred.

The act of completion, as you can see, is vital as it serves as a bridge to the next octave, the next attempt. In anything you do, peak efficiency is really reached when you don't just "finish" something, but complete it. Completion involves setting the stage for the next attempt. In preparing a meal, completion would be fully restoring the kitchen to its "ready" condition for the preparation of the next meal.

Total visual feedback, all the way to completion, is valuable in activities involving physical action, balls, and targets because the feedback received is stored away and utilized in future attempts. Our memories are complete and holographic, and all data is permanently stored and can be accessed consciously and subconsciously. Most of the time, our every move is a creation of the new and utilization of the old and is simply the transcendence and inclusion that is evolution.

Human Potential, Human Performance— What Are the Limits?

How fast can man run? How high can he jump, and how far? How deep can he dive, and how high can he climb? Evolution, it seems, provides the adjustments needed to extend our every capability. The only necessary catalysts seem to be goals. If we set our sights with focused *intention,* we continue to better ourselves in everything that we do, from running faster and faster hundred-yard dashes to creating faster and smaller computers. But can we ever raise the bar beyond our reach? Are there ultimate limits to our vast potential? The only answer can be *no,* unless the concept of infinity is abandoned. The hundred-yard dash world record has reached below nine seconds, and it's only a matter of time until a faster, stronger athlete runs it in a hundredth of a second less, and then another, and another. . . .

Some even *minor* evolutionary changes have taken thousands, even millions, of years, so that, at times, it seems that we've leveled out. But in the big picture, the never-ending march of evolution—the march of transcendence and inclusion—continues. Every existing "record" will eventually be eclipsed, some slowly and others more quickly, but the march will continue. Theorizing along these lines, we look to a future with astounding possibilities. Perhaps some day, in a million years, a runner somewhere will line up for the hundred-yard dash, trying to beat the world record of 1/1,000th of a second. The gun goes off, and before the human ear hears the crack of the pistol shot, the runner is standing at the finish line, having "arrived" there almost simultaneously with the sound. He made it from start to finish using *intention* alone.

Perhaps that is the ultimate destination of evolution—to experience the universe omnisciently within the realm of our own consciousness and within our own context. Distance in space is relative. It is dependent on and determined by time. To illustrate this, consider a drive from New York to Los Angeles. This 3,000-mile cross-country trip, averaging 60 MPH, could be made in about 60 hours, with stops. In a commercial jetliner, the trip is about 6 hours. On the Concorde, it is 2 hours, and on the space shuttle, perhaps 25 minutes. Now, let's take the progression further, increasing the speed and reducing the time of the trip. At 12,000 MPH the trip takes 15 minutes; at 24,000 MPH, 7.5 minutes; and at 48,000 MPH, less than 4 minutes. You can see where the progression leads. At a fast enough speed, the time required to travel between two points in space vanishes to nothing, and *all* places become the same place. And this same place is what our consciousness experiences as the present moment from the standpoint of our own context. In other words, everything that you experience is happening—but from *your* point of view.

CHAPTER 5

Beyond the Zone: From Theory to Practice

In Deepak Chopra's book, *How to Know God,* the gap between science and religion is narrowed. Especially taken with Candace Pert's groundbreaking *Molecules of Emotion,* we are left at the doorstep of the ultimate mystery, namely, what is the source of our reality, of our world, and of the seemingly infinite worlds that we have yet to discover.

As ever-smaller particles of matter are observed and measured, quantum physicists know that at some point solid matter dissolves into empty space, but this "empty space" is not really empty. It is a swirling soup of energy, which on the direction of some unknown force joins and forms itself into shapes of solid matter, in endless variation. Hence the material world that we know as reality.

But what is the intelligence behind these formations, and in particular those that result in *us*—intelligent, conscious beings, possessed of logic and will, beings capable of probing their own origins? Gurdjieff said that everything is mathematics, that is, chemicals and *substances.* And Pert, in the laboratories of hard science, found and is still finding the chemical basis of human emotion, in the form of neuropeptides and their receptors.

But in the gaps between neurons, the *synaptic clefts,* what forces direct the intelligent action of these substances? Gurdjieff spoke of a creating intelligence, and Pert says that perhaps God is in the gaps, the unseen orchestrator of intelligent action. Deepak Chopra says the same, that in the swirling cosmic soup of unseen forces, a universal, guiding force must be at work.

So that is where we are left, in the middle of this void, with nothing left to measure—*nothing* to understand. Only able to theorize, we wait for technological advance. And as it turns out, our knowledge has provided us only with more fuel for faith.

Faced with this sudden dead end, traditional science finds itself more accepting of the study of subtle energies, and the frustrated empiricists are beginning to embrace and chant mantras for new direction. Meanwhile, the subtle-energy theorists, desperate for empirical vindication, seek to forge new technological advances sympathetic to their search. When the subtle energies can be observed and studied, the gap, the void—the swirling soup of cosmic substances—will undoubtedly reveal the nature of God.

To speed the search along, there first must be a shift in not only the consciousness of people in general and influential pockets of people in particular (headed already for a point of critical mass), but there must also be a wholesale shift in the thrust of scientific search and inquiry. We're looking "out" into the cosmos, and we're looking "inward" into the quantum world, but all we're finding is the very same thing—the same substances in infinite combinations, all orbiting other combinations of substances and each being orbited by others as well. Gurdjieff said that by studying ourselves we could study the whole universe: as above, so below. And that, perhaps, is the key. That is why the work of scientists like Pert (and more importantly the publication of it) is so important.

At the end of Chopra's book, the tone is one of resignation, that the human mind is restricted from understanding the unknown. But why have this tone of resignation now—on what could be the brink of discovery?

As above, so below is the most basic and profound Universal Law. In an infinite universe, everything is equally infinite, and this includes the human mind and its potential for discovery. As we come to know what we consider now to be unknowable, the human quest will turn toward itself, and the knowledge of the "mysteries" will serve as a conscious shock to right the veering trajectory of human evolution. Our quest is one of survival.

As we saw earlier, the loop of technological advance/destruction continues until something changes the trajectory—a "conscious shock" in Gurdjieffian terms. If these premises are accurate, and all of the cutting-edge evidence from virtually *every* direction suggests that they are, then the entire human thrust should be to aid the quest for discovery. And this is where the shift from theory to practice begins.

In this section we will explore directions for this shift and see how each individual soul on Earth can and must play a part in this discovery. Actively joining this shift in *human intention* will result in not only an acceleration of the species as a whole, but of the participating individual as well.

As for the zone—think of God as the receptor for human perfection, yourself as the informational neuropeptide, and the zone as the gap between, the gap where the fertile ground enables the search to narrow and ultimately find success. Those fleeting, elusive zone experiences are just a step removed from the Source.

As we've explored the zone, we've come to see that it is a transition space, a springboard to our highest nature. The zone is where matter starts to become finer, as it moves toward dissolution. We can look at matter as a dense construct of finer, unseen energies, seeded with the task of working its way back to the higher state of its origin. Armed with every necessary ingredient for its successful return, it nonetheless must use those ingredients properly. It must, through conscious development of its total being, work to become finer, in all of its dimensions, or centers.

Zone experiences accelerate as this journey back proceeds, experiences such as synchronicity, insight, and extraordinary functioning. *Desire to serve* becomes more important as the ego's density dissolves. So the zone is not so much a thing to *attain* as it is a signpost on the journey back to the Source.

Evolutionary Scouts: Answering the Call

When is it time to join the search? After all, there are no formal recruiters. How do you begin to contribute to this ultimate quest? There are no "study guides."

The call has already come to you, in the form of all the chaos within and around you. As you look out at the world today, you have to agree that this world is in trouble. Many feel that events are totally out of control and that our leaders can do no more than paper the cracks while the edifice of human society on this Earth is falling apart. We are accustomed to seeking expert advice when we are up against a problem we cannot solve; but here it is the experts themselves who are defeated. We look in vain for effectual leadership from politicians, economists, scientists, psychologists, historians, or philosophers.

Theory and practice are equally at sea. We neither see what can be done on the global scale nor do we put into operation commonsense measures, the need for which is obvious to everyone. For all our bluffing, we know we have lost our way. Mankind will continue to flounder until the sheer pressure of events forces us to change our way of living or until there is an act of God that is beyond our understanding.

We cannot readily accept the thought that the course of events is already out of control because we can see that commonsense actions that are technically possible could remove many of our troubles. The universal acceptance of a static economy related to needs rather than greed has been so earnestly advocated by good and influential people that we might have expected governments and people to make at least a small move toward it. We continue to do just the opposite, and this is the crux of the matter. Our ignorance is exceeded only by our impotence.

In the 1920s Gurdjieff came to the West with his message of transformation, saying that man is a machine with no will, no "I," no consciousness and that "he cannot do." The truth of this is becoming so obvious that even professional optimists are beginning to see it. But the full message of transformation is not taken: Man as he is cannot do and he has no will, no consciousness; but he has the potential for becoming a "real man." Those who are in power are unable to do even what is obviously needed, because neither they nor those whom they rule are more than "machines" that can behave only as they are conditioned to do. It is useless to preach to machines, or to encourage or frighten them: they continue to function according to their own mechanical pattern. This is how it is with mankind and will continue to be until our evolution has gone a long way farther.

Some people have learned tricks that can be played with human machines and so gain power over them, but as long as they themselves remain machines, their power is worse than useless. We can see this in the manipulation of public opinion by those who know the tricks. As Gurdjieff put it, "people can be made to believe any old tale and frothing at the mouth will set themselves to convince others that it is so and cannot be otherwise."

Neither the tricksters nor the tricked can see or do anything that they are not conditioned to do by their heredity, upbringing, environment, and fundamental egoism. "Conscious" people (and their numbers are rapidly growing) differ from "experts in manipulation" by their ability to see the reality of the situation, by their freedom from egoism, and by their ability to cooperate with each other. These people are in contact with the higher wisdom, the higher intelligence that surveys life on this Earth as a whole—where it's been and where it might go.

At this moment in human history the question of a higher intelligence, and its possible nature, has become supremely important. If you care to answer this question in the negative, you must agree that our chances for survival for more than the next one or two hundred years is doubtful. Some say that if we can surmount the difficulties of the next twenty or thirty years, the twenty-first century of the Christian Era will see the triumph of man over nature and a world society that will regulate human life in such a way as to eliminate poverty, war, famine, disease, and even, perhaps, death itself. Such predictions are indeed confidently being made by "experts" in "futurology."

But a realistic prediction that takes into account the basic facts of human nature leads to just the opposite conclusion. Every technological advance creates three problems for every one it solves. Every increase in man's power over nature results in more destruction. Human society is not moving toward the brotherhood of man but toward worse manifestations of human selfishness and greed.

We have survived the twentieth century; but unless there are great changes, we will be lucky to survive into the twenty-second. So the conclusion is that there is no way out unless human nature can be changed. For this to occur, direction must come from a higher source of intelligence, one with the potential for influence over us—one whose direction we would follow in blind faith. It must come from an influence such as God.

As Deepak Chopra says, "God has performed the amazing feat of being worshipped and invisible at the same time." And God is worshipped *universally.* In some polls, up to *96 percent* of people believe in God, that unknowable but obviously present higher intelligence *occupying the gaps* that are at the heart of "matter," from where it directs the formations of life and realities. Since all "solid" particles are just concentrations of energies (or intelligent information) in various combinations of substances, then the only true reality is the reality of an infinite "gap," or void.

So God, then, is literally everywhere and in everything. There is, ultimately, nothing *but* God, if that's what we choose to call this directing force. New and greater meaning is suddenly attached to the familiar words, "God is in everyone."

And so with this step, this next bold yet logical step forward, we enter, finally, God's Kingdom, and what do we find? We find, wherever we look, a reflection of ourselves, with God at the core, emanating from the mirror of our own universally shared substances. In this section we will explore the implications of this and form the outline of a plan for using this knowledge to streamline our own evolution, and break free from the endless loop of construction/destruction that has gone unabated for millions of years. This loop has been at its own mercy, on a repeating trajectory that only an appropriate conscious shock can deflect upward. With a critical mass of consciousness on this planet within our grasp, that conscious shock is possible—it is aimed and primed. But we must seize the moment and not let go.

The millennium change, with its attendant awareness of "something more" resonating throughout mankind, is the perfect time. And the teachers, the leaders, are in place. Through *informed intention* we can literally shape, out of that swirling cosmic soup, a new reality, a new trajectory for man. Instead of spending energy in search of God and the mysteries, we can focus that considerable and formidable energy on informed intention, thus clarifying our goals and directing our efforts toward supporting man's continued upward trajectory.

It's been said for many years, and has become sort of a mantra of hopeless surrender, that man only uses a small part of his potential—a tiny amount of his possible powers. And that has been true due to the misdirection and wasting of his energies.

The recent scientific research on prayer and its effects validates the power of intention, especially collective intention. Most of the studies exhibiting dramatic, positive effects involve collective prayer, which can supply informed intent whereas individual prayer may lack this. The increased intention of a group (think of it as a neuropeptide) simply provides a stronger signal as it sniffs out the appropriate receptor (the molecules of the object of the prayer), so that a new action is initiated. In most cases, a healing scenario on a cellular level begins. When individual prayer goes "unanswered," it's because a weak signal—from lack of focus or information—fails to unleash the neuropeptide messenger.

The stimulation of the energies in the "cosmic soup" can only be initiated by a high intelligence—one that is highly focused, one that is informed. Dense, earthly, unconscious influences can never act as the driven frequency. This is why throughout religious literature, and even in modern accounts of healings and "miracles," unexplained acts seem always to be performed by saints, mystics, and consciously evolved masters of esoteric disciplines. Their "thought energy" is refined and highly developed, and it is always highly informed through intense and long-term study. Also, long-term meditation practices as well as other mind-quieting methods enable practitioners to attain altered states of consciousness conducive to *clear focus, more complete learning,* and *thought-control abilities*—all necessary factors for effective prayer.

Since prayer can be looked at as communicating with God—the Source, higher intelligence, or whatever you wish to call the creating and guiding force in the universe—then how we conduct it should be our greatest concern, our highest priority. Quite simply, if we are effective in this communication, then we can tap into the highest source of wisdom and love. And armed with this rarified knowledge, we can conduct our lives in ways that enable us to evolve to the highest possible level—the level of perfection. We can rejoin the intelligence and wonder of the interconnected cosmic soup, and be a part of the orchestration and direction of the greatest symphony of all, the symphony of life.

The Seven Steps to Effective Prayer

As we've seen, effective prayer cannot be whimsical. To be effective, and the latest scientific research says that it can, it must be of a certain quality.

Beginning with the unconscious state, with an energy system of high density and slow vibration, the ground, secretly, is fertile for development. And quite often, paradoxically, from this seemingly barren ground, a turn toward grace is often precipitated by the apparent lack of hope. As the energy collapses on itself, and the light appears to dim, a spark in reserve can ignite a flame of resurgence, and a new growth can begin. This new growth, if properly nurtured, can take the system all the way to God.

Here are the seven steps to effective prayer:

1. Lost in chaos, nowhere to turn
2. A cry for help, recognizing the need
3. Finding a path, committing to break free
4. Evolving the self, working on one's centers
5. Forming intention, mobilizing thought energy
6. Gathering knowledge, informed intention
7. Sending the prayer, overnighting your package to God

We will explore these steps one by one, and you will then have a clear blueprint for your *possible future.*

1. Lost in Chaos, Nowhere to Turn

Many lives today are in chaos, and not only in pockets of society racked by crime and violence. Chaos reigns supreme in upscale neighborhoods, mansions of the wealthy, and even hidden behind the walls of royalty. Chaos has no racial, gender, or socioeconomic preference. Personal turmoil does not search demographics for its victims. And a calm outward appearance cannot conceal the truth of inner storm. As the ratchet of progress tightens, and technological advance shines its light on everything *but the individual,* the individual inevitably finds himself looking into a mirror, and wonders who it is that stares back with empty eyes.

2. A Cry for Help, Recognizing the Need

Suddenly, all of the *things* around him lose significance. He wonders who he is, why he feels empty, and what the future holds for *him*. He thinks, "When did I last laugh like a child?" And he wonders what there could be to laugh about. He thinks, "When did I last love?" And he wonders what there is to love. And he thinks, "When did I last pray?" And he wonders, "How? And to whom?" The mirror he faces may have been thrust in front of him by tragedy or failure, or as a result of his weakness. Facing a devastating loss, with nowhere else to turn, he may have sought its silent reflection as a refuge.

3. Finding a Path, Committing to Break Free

That reflection serves as an honest self-appraisal, and the visual confirmation of his hidden inner state can be the catalyst he needs to break the cycle—the appropriate conscious shock that deflects trajectory.

Whatever form the awakening takes, and sadly for many it never occurs, it usually results in many life changes. Attention to one's self increases, in areas such as diet, exercise, and intellectual and spiritual development. Often, there is a change of friends and even life partners, of geographical location, and of profession. Often, a mentor appears out of nowhere, from the least likely of places, to guide with knowledge and wisdom. These changes signal a different life trajectory, and when rising out of turmoil the new direction is not only warranted but welcomed.

The importance of a trusted mentor cannot be overstated. To have the benefit of an evolved soul's wisdom is incalculable in terms of worth. A mentor can streamline one's personal blueprint for development and provide light when one stumbles into darkness.

Sometimes, the mentor can take surprising form. You never know the level of someone's evolution, especially when you don't know what you're looking for.

4. Evolving the Self, Working on One's Centers

Now committed to a path, and armed with the enthusiasm

of possible positive change, the awakening student, like a curious child, eagerly soaks up everything encountered by the senses. But this child has a blossoming "sixth" sense, *intuition,* which when added to the mix receives information of a refined nature.

To evolve oneself, one must work on and develop all three of his main centers simultaneously: physical, emotional, and intellectual. To work on only one or two would result in an imbalance of energy, and the ability to focus with full clarity would be impaired. Optimum energy can only exist with equal center development. Now let's look at each center separately, and the methods for development.

The physical, or moving center. The physical center involves the body—its health and fitness. To work on this center means to pay conscious attention to these areas on a daily basis, working to maintain and improve both continually. Regarding diet, the latest word from the scientific front points specifically at acid vs. alkaline. A diet too acidic builds up toxins in the body, eventually leading to disease. But when the alkaline/acid ratio is kept at 80 percent/20 percent, toxic buildup cannot occur, and the organism thrives. In addition, a *balanced* diet is always a good idea, as long as the acid/alkaline ratio is kept in mind.

Personal hygiene falls into the health category and is an extremely important contributing factor.

Regular medical checkups can prevent problems coming "out of nowhere."

The body needs adequate water around the clock. Water shortage in the body means less efficiency on a cellular level, and the cells of the body need to be continually "bathed" in water. For added caution, drink water that has been alkalized.

When a person decides to abuse substances such as drugs, tobacco, and alcohol, he is abusing his own body—not a very conscious thing to do.

So health is one part of a developed physical center and is most likely achieved through proper nourishment, regular attention to hygiene, regular as well as preventative upkeep (medical monitoring), hydration, and avoidance of substance abuse. Also important to the development of the physical center is keeping the body fit, and this ties in of course to health. Fitness is achieved through regular exercise, which prevents the muscular and skeletal structure from atrophying due to disuse.

Stretching, walking at a brisk pace, and perhaps even a regular routine of light weight training is enough to maintain a healthy level of fitness. A body that is unused will deteriorate rapidly, leading to inefficient functioning of its systems. Manual labor, *done consciously,* is a terrific way to work on the physical center and has other benefits as well.

Done consciously means done in the spirit of personal benefit, not in the spirit of resentment or distaste. And when you know that you are doing something that is for your benefit, it's a good feeling. We now know that "good feelings" are synonymous with good chemicals—good substances—and good energy.

All this adds up to an evolution of the entire energy system—the one we call ourselves. Zen masters would say that if you have to sweep a floor, try to do the best floor-sweeping job in the history of the world, every time you do it. This attitude will refine the very substances of your being and will also keep you in the present, with focused attention. This is good practice for what comes later.

The emotional, or feeling center. Working on the emotional center involves, among other things, freeing up feelings. All of the emotions must be expressed, or trouble will follow. To quote Pert's *Molecules of Emotion,* in which she reveals, from the hallowed halls of empirical science, the chemical basis for all human functioning, including feelings, "My research has shown me that when emotions are expressed—which is to say that the *biochemicals* [the neuropeptides and their appropriate receptors] *that are the substrate of emotion* are flowing freely—all systems are united and made whole. When emotions are repressed, denied, not allowed to be whatever they may be, our network pathways get blocked, stopping the flow of the vital feel-good, unifying chemicals that run both our biology and our behavior." And Pert has more to say about the relationship of emotions and health. "The neuropeptides and their receptors are the substrates of the emotions, *and they are in constant communication with the immune system,* the mechanism through which health and disease are created."

When the feel-good chemicals are not flowing freely, that is, when they are blocked or repressed, then the communication breaks down, and the immune system is *less informed.* In the resulting state of confusion, many of the feel-bad chemicals (dormant cancer cells, free radicals, etc.) have free rein. Put simply, nonexpression of the emotions causes depression and disease.

In Gurdjieff's incredible three-centered work, an important part of the system is the intentional instigation of emotional release. His students did much work on their emotional centers. It could be one reason why most of his serious pupils lived far beyond the life expectancy of the times.

There are many healthy and practical ways to stimulate the emotions, but it is extremely important to remember that *honesty* must prevail when dealing with human feeling. Self-honesty—keeping your word to others as well as to yourself—allows you to live in a state of personal integrity. When you don't operate this way, when you are at cross purposes, the emotions become confused. There is a lack of emotional integrity, and physiologic integrity is likewise altered.

Art is a powerful and enjoyable way to stimulate the emotions. As we have already discussed, objective art, especially, is a strong and predictable stimulant. Music and literature, including poetry, are accessible and fun ways of healthily experiencing emotion. Every day at The Prieure, Gurdjieff's school outside of Paris, music (his and Thomas De Hartmann's own compositions of objective music, played by De Hartmann) and dance were experienced and practiced. Music should be a part of your daily life, for it elevates mood, evokes emotional response, and has the power to calm—all very beneficial effects.

Read literature that inspires you or sparks creativity. Happy, inspirational material can elicit the same qualities in the reader.

And don't forget to dance. While working the physical center, dancing also releases endorphins, the feel-good chemicals. Dancing is good for the body and the soul. It is literally a playground for the emotions.

Sadness is every bit as important an emotion as joy, as blockage of either is detrimental to our health. Don't stifle grief. You need to express it when appropriate and necessary.

A good cry—like a good laugh—can cleanse the spirit, and on a physiological scale ensure the free flow of chemicals in the body. When this flow is blocked, all sorts of miscommunications are caused among the body's life-regulating systems. And just as in the world of human relationships, miscommunication is the harbinger of misunderstanding. When the vital systems of the body are unable to communicate freely, balance is lost and chaos rules.

The intellectual, or thinking center. Just as the body and emotions must be strengthened and informed, so must the mind and its process of thinking and knowing. A mind that is exposed to minimal learning and little stimulation will atrophy much like the muscles in a paralyzed leg.

The development of the intellectual center includes study of each of the centers and knowledge of how they operate and how to operate them consciously. The methods are self-observation (including study of the body), study of Universal Laws, and study of human psychology. We have already discussed Universal Laws—the Law of Three and the Law of Seven, the overseeing law of as above, so below, and some of the other governing laws of the physical universe such as the Law of Orbit. We have also discussed self-observation at length, and have touched on human psychology, and how it is guided and shaped by honesty and conscience.

The intellectual center is about learning and knowledge, especially self-knowledge, for in a world where as above, so below holds true, we can study the whole universe simply by studying ourselves. Another part of your daily schedule should include the gathering and assimilation of knowledge—of yourself and of universal law.

5. *Forming Intention, Mobilizing Thought Energy*

You've been to the depths—for each of us they're at different levels—and yet you survived. You've been roused from your sleep, by some life event with impact. And now you've committed to ascend from the depths and reach new heights, and you've found a path.

With all you've learned, it now is time to enlist the help that's always been there, buried under layers of illusion and ego. It's time to involve your essence, with its direct line to the Source of information and intelligence, in your quest for a soul. Gurdjieff said that we are not born with a soul, only the substances from which one can be developed. With the right work, and the resultant states of truth and objective conscience, that soul material can be fashioned into an immortal "spirit body," one that rejoins the cosmic dance and becomes part of the Source from which it came.

By taking human form—a lower frequency, a denser state—to fulfill cosmic purpose (read Gurdjieff's "All and Everything"), that soul material has set before it a task, part of which is to refine its frequency and density and then return to its true home in the infinite, swirling soup of cosmic energy and light. The task ahead is simple. It is to live in objective truth and increase constantly your level of vibration through work on your three main centers, and to help those around you to do the same. It is to help transmute negative energy wherever possible, and to help spread the truth of Universal Laws. And finally, it is to love others unconditionally by always recognizing and accepting the level of consciousness from which they operate.

When you decide to do something, you have an *intention*. This intention can be a weak, non-urgent impulse, or it can take the form of a burning desire. Which of the two are you most likely to fulfill?

The stronger the intention, the greater the concentration of "thought energy," and the greater chance for effect. When intention reaches the stage of a "burning desire," its beam can be laserlike in its purity of focus. The intention can turn into a complete visualization—with imagery—of not only the intended process, but of the successful end result of the process.

When the beam of intention is pure, it rides the waves of energy as it streaks toward its completion point. And all the while, the chemicals of the intention, the *neuropeptides,* bind with their receptors and enable the physical process to occur.

There is a gap between the material world and the nonmaterial world of thought. But we now know that there is a material substrate of the world of thought, the neuropeptide molecules and their receptor molecules—the "informational messengers" of the body—and we propose that intention is the bridge between those worlds. But it is a certain kind and quality of intention.

Intention can take countless forms. It can be, as we've said, a casual fleeting thought, it can be—much farther up the scale—a burning desire, and it can be a clear-focused, informed intention of stunning clarity and power. The neuropeptides influenced by thought energy can be barely stirred (by the casual thought), they can be primed for action and sent sniffing out for receptors (by the burning desire), or they can be sent streaking toward their receptors, binding quickly, surely, and completely, thus actualizing the thought of intention. The latter is the result of the intention's clarity of focus as well as its depth of information.

In other words, the intention was clear, and it was well informed. What does *informed intention* mean? Let's explore this question as we move ever closer to communicating—on Earthly terms—with God.

6. *Gathering Knowledge, Informed Intention*

As the number of neuropeptide molecules involved in the

search for their receptors increase, the number of "bindings" increase, and so the number of informed cells start to do their job—the job of congregating in such ways as to cause physical action.

It is important that the information carried by the messenger molecules, via thought energy, is as specific to the intention as possible. They must consider the implications for all three centers, so that the information they carry to their receptors, which ultimately will inform the object cells to act, is as complete as possible. Keep in mind that thought energy, which lies between the world of matter and the network of interconnected universal energy, is capable of delivering messages and information *both ways*. So if the thought energy includes and considers all implications of a resulting action, then the intention is highly informed.

Also, due to the universal Law of Seven, only intentions of an ascending evolutionary nature have the possibility of unfettered actualization. Let's go through an example of the process. First let's state the Law of Intention: *For an action to take place that fulfills the object of an intention, the cells of the material body must receive static-free signals—they must be well informed—from the informational cells that form the thoughts.*

Sarah decides that she wants to become a better tennis player. She inquires about lessons at her club and, after determining the cost, books a series of lessons with the tennis professional. Her lessons are set for Mondays, Wednesdays, and Fridays for three weeks. She knows that there will be possible conflicts with this schedule but figures that she can "work it out."

Note that, already, the intention is weakened by possible interruptions and stressful conflicts, and therefore the quality of her actions will be diluted.

Sarah has two young children, one of whom is not yet in school. She typically juggles school carpool duty with housework, grocery shopping, cooking, mothering, being a wife, social schedules, and personal chores. Her once-a-week tennis game is more social and casual than serious, so her decision (intention) to improve her game appears whimsical considering the circumstances. And committing to nine lessons, knowing that will cause many logistical problems, sabotages the intention right from the start.

If Sarah had sat down with her intention in the formative stage, and considered all of the implications of the decision, she would have seen that perhaps the intention could be better formed and acted on at a later, more convenient time. The "three-center examination" would have revealed that at the physical level, she was not a serious enough player to warrant a series of nine lessons at this time, given her other priorities; at the emotional level she would end up feeling rushed and guilty for neglecting priorities to satisfy a whim; and at the intellectual level the time and expense made no sense. It would have revealed that this pursuit could perhaps be made at a more convenient time in her life.

In any case, Sarah started her series of lessons. After some initial enthusiasm, the thrill began to wane. She had to cancel the third lesson due to a first-grade function that she just "couldn't miss." And weather forced cancellation of the fourth lesson, after which her tennis game was worse than ever, and she felt that she had to "start all over again." She took one more lesson on a day when she should have been doing other, more important things, and so her mind just wasn't "with it." That lesson was Sarah's last, and so she ended up paying for nine lessons that she didn't take and was left with lowered self-esteem and a "still bad" tennis game. Sarah's intention, to play better tennis, was never realized.

On the other hand, Sarah's sister Kathy decided to take a gardening class at the local university. Kathy loved to work in the garden; it was her passion. Kathy was married, with one small child at home. She approached her husband, Jim, to get his opinion on her intention. She had already researched the cost and the days and times of classes and had figured out how to arrange things so that her classes would not interfere much with their normal schedules.

Jim, knowing Kathy's love of gardening, and himself appreciating the beautiful landscaping of their home, due to Kathy's effort, creativity, and talent, supported her decision wholeheartedly, and even volunteered to help with the duties that her classes would infringe upon. This support from Jim made Kathy *feel good* about her decision, and she made plans with a clear mind and a happy heart. Knowing that the logistics were manageable erased any possibility of stress, and she looked forward to the course, which would include hands-on work in the dirt, as well as textbook learning about the art and science of gardening. All three of Kathy's centers were accounted for in positive ways and would be developed further by the experience.

Kathy's intention was clear and focused, unclouded by doubt. It was also heavily informed, with consideration and attention to all three centers. Thus Kathy was free to pursue the completion of her intention, happily and pressure free. And she did. Her intention became reality, resulting in an ascending evolution of her three main centers.

7. Sending the Prayer, Overnighting Your Package to God

First of all, we have to gently move away from the notion of God as a white-haired figure, sitting on a golden chair suspended above the clouds. This schoolbook image implants in the mind an unknowable figure that cannot be intellectually reconciled. In reality, all indications from the cutting edge of modern science (the holographic theory, quantum physics, the daily observations of outer space), combined with all discovered traces of ancient teachings and the postulations of history's greatest thinkers, points to the same determination: God is the higher *ordering* intelligence, the source and orchestrator of all energy.

Some ancient teachings call God the Original Emanating and Ever-Expanding Sound or the Infinite Expansion and Illumination of Light. God is the driven frequency. But that begs the question, "Driven by what, or whom?"

This intelligence could be in the form of a super-intelligent energy. Whatever the form, God is a source that we are capable of contacting, tapping into, and receiving signal and direction from. It's proven every day in the form of miracles, events that are unexplained by any Earthly convention.

There is no question that there *is* a higher order of reality. How else can one explain a child of three sitting at the piano for the first time and playing perfect Mozart? How can one explain an idiot savant performing mathematical calculations faster than the fastest computer—and at the same time being incapable of spelling his name?

These things happen, and it is evident that a higher order of energy is at work, an order normally inaccessible. And if you say that it's simply a random, more perfected configuration of chemicals (energy) in the brain, then you're saying that such perfected configurations exist. A perfected configuration of energy—perhaps that is what we should call God.

So taking as a very educated premise the concept of God as an energy, whether sound, light, or white-haired man, that energy would be connected in some way to all other energies. This understood, it only remains to find the connective devices or substances that reach across spectrums of energy of diverse densities and vibrations.

The study of subtle energies explores those realms, where matter dissolves and where nonmaterial energy "solidifies," on the direction of an informed and purposeful God. Yet even this new matter imparts its will and *information* so that it can work its way back to its source, more informed (further evolved) for the effort. Such is the play of God, to create, observe, and oversee an ascending evolution.

Now we're at the stage where exciting things happen, where "miracles" can occur. The intention (or prayer) is formed. The focus is clear, undiluted by doubt or fear. The intention is informed, educated by the consideration of the three main human centers, and armed with the forethought of all possible implications of actualization. The package is wrapped, ready to send. What happens next?

Meditation for Delivery

Find a comfortable, peaceful place and let yourself relax. Give yourself time to fully relax your body *and* your thoughts. Just rest in the Witness while every part of your body relaxes and sinks into a restful space.

When you feel your consciousness beginning to change, when the beta waves subside and the alpha state approaches, just before sleep, bring your intention to mind, visualizing with imagery, involving the senses. *See* the result of your intention, *feel* it, *hear* it, *taste* it, or *smell* it. Let the image of your fulfilled intention linger in your mind. And just at the moment when the image is most clear, when light illuminates the space around it in your mind's eye, hold the image as if in freeze frame, and visualize the messenger molecules in your body that are the chemical correlates of your thoughts, and of your intentions. Visualize those specific molecules gathering, mobilizing, and then streaking off throughout the body to join with their receptors, all in a flash of thought, and imagine them binding all at once as they initiate a symphony of action that only ends when your intention has become reality.

What you've just done is what philosophers and scientists have explored for centuries. It is what they've wondered and theorized about since the myth of the parting of the Red Sea. It is mind over matter. Is it possible? When your prayer is answered, or when synchronicity is revealed, or when your child spontaneously plays Mozart, you will know, intuitively, the answer.

A strong clue lies in placebo studies, where subjects are able to change their cell counts, heart rates, body temperatures, and many other physiological states and measures, all while taking a sugar pill and being told that it is medication that will bring about the desired effect. This is the power of expectation, the working part of intention. Let's explore the power of expectation a bit further, in order to complete our study of the secrets of communicating with God.

The Power of Expectation

There is a vast difference between *having confidence* and

expecting. Having confidence is an *empty construct of language*. It means "I *think* I can do this." It is strictly intellectual and not rooted in "feeling." It's a one-center characteristic. Although a valuable asset, confidence is *denser* than expectation; it has a *lower vibration*. It is not as energetic. And so its influence is not as strong. You might say that it is farther from the Absolute or perfection.

Expectation, however, is altogether different. Expectation has a finer energy, a higher vibratory wave. Much like true prayer, it is not *asking*, but *affirming*. Put another way, having confidence is simply believing that it is possible for something to happen. But an expectation is *feeling and sensing that it will*. You must first have confidence, and then you must have the expectation.

And now comes the big question that you are ready to ask. How does one go about having an expectation? How can you *make yourself* expect something?

The answer is long, but if you're willing to follow, we'll lead you there. The answer begins with *energy*. As we have stated, as things move up toward the Absolute, their vibrations become faster, their densities finer, and their energies greater and more pure, thereby gaining more potential for positive influence on surrounding matter.

With our senses, we receive impressions from the world, from this vast and varied energy field. The impressions that we sense—that we see, hear, feel, taste, smell, and intuit—determine our course. And the energy that we process is of differing frequencies.

If we process mostly high density, low energy impressions, then we are likely to follow low-energy pathways of action via our three centers. We are likely to *move* with low energy, *feel* with low energy, and *think* with low energy. The results are usually negative.

To see this process in action, simply contrast the impressional influences on man #1, the educated man who has a solid family background, has a good job, enjoys good health, has some form of faith, and is surrounded by a supportive, loving family, with man #2, the addicted and impoverished criminal who wallows in the deep end of society's cesspool, alone, miserable, uneducated, and hopeless. How many negative impressions does man #1 encounter and process compared with man #2? Ask yourself, where does the energy come from, and what are the results of the impressions received?

In all of life, in order to produce positive results, one must *expect* them. And in order to expect them, one must process information in such a way as to increase the energy of one's centers, so that they can then direct that energy toward *energetic action*. And energetic action can be defined as *action with expectation.*

Our three main centers must work as one, blending in unison the energy fed to them by the senses. When they do, we feel, think, and act with an abundance of positive energy. We feel confident, we think expectantly, and we act efficiently.

Choosing Impressions

The key to expecting, as you can see, is in the energy quality of the impressions that we process. Once we know how to determine that quality, we can *focus attention*—our senses—on the appropriate impressions. However, the energy quality of an impression depends on the context in which it is perceived. We'll give you an example.

Ordinarily, a tree and a lake would be considered objects of positive energy. They are miracles of nature, peaceful and calming to look at. But on a golf course, for the golfer, it depends. Standing on a teeing area waiting for the group ahead to clear, one can draw energy from focusing attention on a particularly beautiful nearby tree. But the lake that lies ahead, which forces the drive to carry over 200 yards, can cause great fear and suck your energy down in a flood of negative thoughts. Focused on, it almost guarantees disaster. So focusing one's attention on energy sources must be very selective.

Things that "lift" one's spirits, like birds, flowers, and rainbows, are agents of transmutation. To transmute means to "change the nature of," and so transmuting energy means to take in the energy of the impression, consider it in its highest (or most positive) form, and let it *lift* your own energy by incorporating it into your field.

Anything that we encounter with our senses leaves an impression. The extent of the impression is determined by the time of exposure and the depth of the attention, while the quality of the impression is determined by the context—negative or positive—in which it is viewed.

Finding Your Zone: What to Do with the *Rest* of Your Life

This was the name of the seminar in Austin in 1993 where I had gone to meet, and experience the work of, Martin Sage. Sage had contacted me after reading my first book, which had broken new ground by applying principles of the holographic theory to human performance. He wanted to explore the possibilities of working together and wanted me to learn firsthand what his work was about.

I was in for quite a surprise. Sage's method, called the Sage Learning Method, uses immediate video feedback in a group setting, as well as a unique interview process, and the results of his work are remarkable. Sage is literally moving flesh. Let me explain.

He begins by filming, with both a video and a 35mm camera, each side of your face separately. Then the people in your group, typically six to eight individuals, look at the films, one side of the face at a time. The group, one by one, is asked to comment on what they see, not opinions or stories, but short, descriptive comments such as joy, sadness, right eye closed or dark, left eye full of light, and so on.

Well, if you're in psychotherapy and the therapist makes an observation of this kind, it's easy to stay in denial and argue, one on one. After all, it's only one person's opinion. But when eight people all look at a close-range picture of the right side of your face and your right eye, and tell you collectively and unanimously that they see sadness or no light, or that the eye is closed and "dead," it has great impact.

After this process is over, with both sides of the face having been examined and analyzed by the instructor and the group, the interviewing process begins, again in front of the group, whose opinions you've now come to value, despite the discomfort and squirming that their observations have caused. The group's instructor, but more often Sage himself, conducts the interview, the purpose of which is to find out what "lights you up"—what your *fascination* is. When your fascination is discovered, it is discussed at length. Sage says that whatever it is that lights you up, someone is making a living at it.

Now you're filmed again, the same way, and the filming/viewing/analysis process is repeated. As you view yourself now, and the group comments on what they see, it is truly incredible to see the physical transformations that occur.

The interview process, which is designed to exercise and stimulate both sides of the face—and both hemispheres of the brain (which control the face)—balances the two sides, with the weaker, unstimulated side matching the "healthier" side. The point is, most people have a great imbalance, with one side or the other not receiving adequate stimulation. Either their creative, imaginative, intuitive (right brain) side is not being used, or their logical, practical, scientific side (left brain) is being neglected. The results show on the corresponding side of the face, and in and around the eyes (left side for right brain, right side for left brain).

Not surprisingly, many of Sage's students decide to change their lives after attending his sessions, especially when they see what their current situations have done to them. They often change professions, learn to be more balanced in their activities, and go on to live healthier, happier, longer lives.

The 1993 seminar/session that I attended had forty-two

participants, and the forty-two people were last filmed an hour or so before the seminar ended Sunday evening. On a large screen, films were shown of each person, the first films that were taken on Saturday prior to the seminar. Next to that picture was shown the last film taken.

Every participant, without exception, looked happy and vibrant, and at least ten to fifteen years younger than when he or she arrived. So Sage is, quite literally, *moving flesh.* And the best part of it is that he gives you the methods to reinforce the changes, so that they stay with you. Couples are shown how to *recharge each other* daily.

It is all quite amazing, really, but it illustrates what we've come to learn about the workings of our minds and bodies. Mind over matter works. Infused with information, and driven by clear and evolutionary (positive) intention, our minds and bodies can draw nearer to God's perfection.

A Theory of Everything

ENERGY—Divine Impulse

1. INFORMATION—Source of Knowledge
2. LOVE—Refines Knowledge

We are now going to use a diagram and text to describe and explain what appears to be a plausible "theory of everything." Based on information gathered at this time, from every available source, exoteric (theoretical), mesoteric (philosophical), and esoteric (hidden knowledge), from the teachings of every known discipline and religion both ancient and modern, and from the frontiers of science, both traditional and nontraditional, you are invited to explore, with an open mind, the possible true nature of your world. The ultimate aim of this knowledge would be for all Earthly beings to evolve the performance of every facet of their lives.

Taking the latest discoveries in science, and including in that ever-broadening yet historically narrow field the research into quantum physics, outer space, and subtle energies, and blending them with interdisciplinary ancient religious teaching, one emerges with a sense of what Trismegistus meant when he proposed *his* theory of everything—his timeless observation, as above, so below. Now, it just happens that the era in which the Egyptian prophet recorded those words is, to us, the distant, unfathomable past. And considering the mounting evidence of earlier advanced technologies, those words could well have been uttered, in some long-lost language, a million years ago.

The words of Trismegistus, like the Sermon on the Mount, are remarkable for their timelessness. As applicable today as when recorded, these teachings qualify as universal law.

Most accepted authenticated early teachings as well as cutting-edge scientific and philosophical theories agree on one important point—that there is a source, if not a creator, of interconnected informational intelligence, characterized by a constant evolutionary movement toward a finer energy (what could be called love), which drives the universe. Congruent to a *theory of everything*, we shall call this source *The Divine Impulse of Energy*. Radiating out from the original emanation in an infinite, eternal, symmetrical spread, this impulse carries energy in two forms as it branches out in seemingly endless variation. Each variation, however, has at its heart the impulse of Divine Energy.

The two forms of the *original energy* are *Information,* the source of life and knowledge, and *Love,* which by entering life refines that knowledge through *intention* and *will.*

Man was not created with the element of Divine Love, and it was the mission of Jesus Christ, according to religious teaching, to transmit through His teachings that missing part of man's makeup—*The Holy Spirit.*

Let's begin by retracing the steps of the evolution of our world, back to its possible beginning, back to the original consciousness. We have no choice but to begin from mystery, even if the mystery itself is that there was no beginning. Even starting from *that* premise, a process was in motion at the time when life as we know it began its evolutionary journey, a journey that we have discovered a great deal about.

So we can take either of two basic premises:

     1. Creation theory—some mysterious entity or energy form started a process, or

     2. Noncreation theory—a process with no beginning or end is simply going on, always has been, and always will be

Regardless of the accepted premise—which *must* begin from mystery—once we enter the progression of evolution there is no denying that there is an ever-expanding "branching out" of the universe—"universe" meaning all that we humans are aware of.

Creation theorists claim that in a noncreation theory there is no place for "a higher intelligence," or "a source of Divine Love," but that is an erroneous assumption. That possibility is only another potential mystery, no different than any other, including those that the creationists base their theories and beliefs on. "God" may have always existed, for instance, but who's to say in what form?

Hypothetically, if God is the "ultimate" energy field, then all movement of that field could result in an infinite "fanning out" of that energy into infinite manifestations. And the coarser manifestations, as the result of certain combinations of substances, could possess certain unique characteristics such as will and conscience—characteristics that would be their only means of transformation back toward their source—and unique levels of consciousness. Already we know, through scientific inquiry, the chemical substrates of things like "thoughts" and "emotions."

Now let's look at the ancient, esoteric knowledge rooted in mathematics and sound: the Universal Laws of Three and Seven. You will recall that the Law of Three states that every phenomenon is the result of the action of three forces: an active (or positive), passive (or negative), and neutralizing force. The higher blends with the lower in order to actualize the middle and thus becomes either higher for the preceding lower, or lower for the succeeding higher.

Examples of *three forces* are everywhere. In Christianity, the three forces represent the Trinity; the Father, the Son, and the Holy Spirit. In Hinduism, they are Brahma, Vishnu, and Shiva. In chemistry, the smallest constituents of matter (atoms) contain three forces: protons, neutrons, and electrons. In atoms, the protons have their own three inner constituents called "quarks." And there are three primary colors, three notes in a chord, and so on. In all things and in all events, we can find the Law of Three.

The enneagram is an ancient universal symbol that embodies all Universal Laws. The circle represents the Oneness, Unity, God, the Absolute; the triangle represents the three independent forces; and the six-pointed figure represents the Law of Seven or the *Law of Vibrations.*

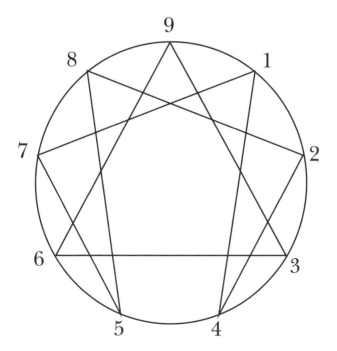

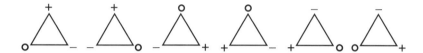

In the Law of Three, six triads, or six combinations, of the three forces are possible. The positive, negative, and neutralizing principles, or three forces, can only manifest through six triads. But ancient esoteric knowledge of a secret nature tells of a seventh triad, one that is only available to the Absolute, *a triad in which the three forces are united.*

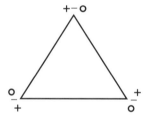

The Law of Seven (or the Law of Octaves or the Law of Vibrations) is the first fundamental law of the universe. This sacred primordial law has seven deflections or, as it is still otherwise said, seven "centers of gravity" and the distance between each two of these deflections or centers of gravity is called an interval.

In the definition of an octave is a restoring "do" (an eighth tone), which is, in reality, the first tone of the next octave. That definition is as follows: "the eighth full tone above a given tone, having *twice* as many vibrations per second, or below a given tone, having *half* as many vibrations per second; also, the *interval of eight diatonic degrees* between a tone and either of its octaves." From this definition, we can easily comprehend two of the main features of this law: a sevenfold structure and a double or half structure.

For example, a musical octave contains seven notes—do-re-mi-fa-so-la-ti. Also, musical octaves always indicate a doubling or halving of vibrations; that is, middle C is at 256 vibrations per second and high C is at 512 vibrations per second.

Other examples of the Law of Seven are the splitting of light through a prism into seven colors; or the rate of decay of radioactive material, which is calculated in terms of its half-life.

Music starts with 1 vibration per second (vps). This doubles to 2 vibrations per second and forms an octave. If we double it to 4 vibrations per second, we create another octave.

If we continue this doubling—8 vps, 16 vps, 32 vps, 64 vps, 128 vps—when we reach 256 vibrations per second we will be at what music defines as middle C. If we double it again to 512 vibrations per second we will be at high C.

These are the basics. Upon them we can effectuate a detailed examination into the diatonic structure (five whole steps, two half-steps) of the octave. Between the initial vibration and either double or half of that vibration, six "additional" diatonic vibrations come into existence. These six vibrations occur at specific ratios, which were first documented by Pythagoras, a sixth century B.C. philosopher and mathematician. These are fittingly called the Pythagorean Harmonies.

DO—the "ascending do" has the value of 1. The other vibrations are increasing ratios of this vibration.

RE—exceeds the vibration of the ascending do by 1/8 (1+1/8), or the ratio 9 to 8 (9/8), or the factor 1.125.

MI—exceeds the vibration of the ascending do by 1/4 (1+1/4), or the ratio 5 to 4 (5/4), or the factor 1.25.

FA—exceeds the vibration of the ascending do by 1/3 (1+1/3), or the ratio 4 to 3 (4/3), or the factor 1.333.

SO—exceeds the vibration of the ascending do by 1/2 (1+1/2), or the ratio 3 to 2 (3/2), or the factor 1.5.

LA—exceeds the vibration of the ascending do by 2/3 (1+2/3), or the ratio 5 to 3 (5/3), or the factor 1.666.

TI—exceeds the vibration of the ascending do by 7/8 (1+7/8), or the ratio 15 to 8 (15/8), or the factor 1.875.

DO—the "descending do" completes the octave and is twice the vibration of the ascending do.

These ratios may be verified by taking a string of convenient length, say 60 inches, on a monochord, tuning it to C, and then successively shortening it in the reciprocals of the figures shown. It will then be found that a length:

of 53.33 inches (60 divided by 9/8) will sound D

of 48 inches (60 divided by 5/4) will sound E

of 45 inches (60 divided by 4/3) will sound F and so on.

Interval:	1	2	3	4	5	6	7	8
Name:	C	D	E	F	G	A	B	C
Frequency Ratio to C:	1	9/8	5/4	4/3	3/2	5/3	15/8	2/1

The relation C to D is the same as the ratio 8 to 9.
The relation C to E is 4 to 5;
C to F is 3 to 4;
C to G is 2 to 3;
C to A is 3 to 5;
C to B is 8 to 15; and
C to its octave is 1 to 2.

The inverse relationship—the frequency to the length of the string—reveals the "diatonic scale."

Diatonic Scale

DO	2 vibrations per second (descending DO)	2
TI	1.875 vps or 1 7/8 or	15/8
LA	1.666 vps or 1 2/3 or	5/3
SO	1.5 vps or 1 1/2 or	3/2
FA	1.333 vps or 1 1/3 or	4/3
MI	1.25 vps or 1 1/4 or	5/4
RE	1.125 vps or 1 1/8 or	9/8
DO	1 vps (ascending DO)	1

To establish a collective understanding, we will call any totality or any part of a totality that conforms to these ratios "diatonic." Any whole phenomenon can be calculated as an octave, as a "something" that runs from its allness to its nothingness, or vice versa, dividing the totality "diatonically" by the ratios: 1/8, 1/4, 1/3, 1/2, 2/3, and 7/8.

The Law of Three and the Law of Seven, taken together within the circle/symbol that is the enneagram, reveal a mathematically based theory that conforms to scientific as well as religious "doctrine." The Law of Three, with an additional (seventh) triad of possible arrangements of the three forces, suggests that when the three forces were separated from the Absolute, creation occurred. This separation, or "explosion," was accompanied by energetic vibrations—of sound and light.

And so the three forces were sent hurtling away from the their Source and into an infinite loop of interaction. This actualizes new creations branching out in a never-ending process—a process that we call evolution.

The three forces—the positive, negative, and neutralizing—are constantly striving to reunite, and in so doing touch off endless new actualizations. Remember the formula—*the higher blends with the lower in order to actualize the middle and thus becomes either higher for the preceding lower, or lower for the succeeding higher.* When the three forces do meet and an act of creation takes place, the neutral force in one event may become the active force in the next event—for the three forces change with respect to one another as they go about spinning or braiding the thread of occurrences.

Now, with each new entity, a new octave begins, and this is where the Law of Seven takes over. Each new actualization, which, as philosopher Ken Wilber states, *transcends and includes* its predecessor, starts its journey. That journey moves along, constantly subject to the two critical intervals. Each time one of those critical intervals is not filled appropriately, the trajectory of the process at hand is deflected.

The Law of Seven governs successions of events. It states that evolution is nonlinear. There is an orderly discontinuity in all progressions and series. And this lawful discontinuity is preserved in our musical scale, which, as singing up and down any octave will show, is composed of unequal steps. Do, re, and mi are equally distant from one another, but between mi and fa there is a half-step instead of a full step. Proceeding up the scale, we have so, la, and ti separated by full intervals, but ti and do have a half-step between them again.

The Law of Seven explains why when something begins it does not just continue and continue, ad infinitum: why a rainstorm abates or a grudge finally loses its venom. And this Universal Law is behind the fact that there are no straight lines in nature. The intervals—the critical junctures within every process—must be filled appropriately (with the occurrence necessary for the continuation of the octave) in order for a process to run to successful completion. And this, for man, is where the three centers come into play, with application of their specific actions resulting from the proper assimilations of the foods for the centers—"food" food, air, and impressions.

Man appears to be unique in the universe. While all other manifestations of energy remain subject to mechanical laws (as does man), and are at the mercy of ever-deflecting trajectories, man can, through his will and intention—through his consciousness—control his trajectories. He can, if he possesses the necessary knowledge, consciously fill the intervals that continuously appear as his every process evolves.

What must remain shrouded in mystery are two important and seemingly unanswerable questions. First, who or what caused the separation of the three unified forces? And second, why, apparently, does man alone possess a *will?*

Combining science, the most reliable and time-tested religious theory, and human logic, the most plausible theory has to be the theory of God. God, for some reason, created the universe. God set in motion events that caused creation.

The way that human evolution has played out so far lends

credence to major religious thought; that man, due to his own free will, has degenerated the purity of his being, despite being created in the image of a perfect God.

And science, for its part, has made great strides in tracing our path through history.

There is no need for science and religion to occupy lonely corners of theory, for as both focuses of inquiry advance, they will come to see that there is no difference. Both must begin from a premise of mystery, and then trace the steps of God's creation.

What is most important for all of us to remember, whether we pitch our tent in the camp of science or religion, is that in either case the universal law of *as above, so below* applies. We are in a position, due to our rapidly accelerating technology and information-spreading capabilities, to literally guide our evolution of consciousness—and more importantly to show our children early on that they can do the same. We should be able, if not in the next decade then certainly by the middle of the twenty-first century, to finally reach a critical mass of conscious people on this Earth, and break free from the endless loop that has become mankind's own samsara.

On Astrology and Numerology

There is much disagreement among contemporary thinkers and visionaries on these topics. Some place great importance on astrological charts and numbers while others relegate astrology and numerology to the categories of fantasy and charlatanism. Numerology, meanwhile, is even less understood and more maligned than astrology.

To be fair, many of the modern-day representations of these "sciences" have turned off vast numbers of people, and these misrepresentations have distorted the true nature of these ancient methods of viewing life.

Gurdjieff once said if you help others, you will be helped, perhaps tomorrow, perhaps in 100 years, but you will be helped. Nature must pay off the debt. It is a mathematical law and *all life is mathematics.*

Anyone who even remotely senses the interrelatedness of all things must surely admit that in a universe that is weblike in nature, that is, a connected, seamless field, the alignment of forces at any given time must influence any new emerging entity. That new entity is literally made up, in part, of the substances of those forces. And these alignments can be reduced, or perhaps a better word would be expanded, to mathematics—numbers. There is no difference between astrology and numerology. They both deal with mathematics, or numbers—their alignment, their quantity, their frequency.

The interpretation of both involves deciphering various alignments and surrounding circumstances, all of which are ultimately reducible to exact mathematical universal law. Either the Law of Three or the Law of Seven can be applied to the final analysis, and from that a predictable, coherent result can be observed.

So the *mathematical alignments* surrounding the points of conception and birth have a great deal to do with the manifestations exhibited by the organism, because the organism is partly comprised of the substances present at those points in time. So *real astrology* and *real numerology* are indeed important ways of looking at the overall makeup of any organism.

The Task of the Indigo Children

The Indigo Children, born into the vortex of the new millennium, inherit from us a legitimate chance for global transformation. (See Lee Carroll and Jan Tober's book, *The Indigo Children.*) Our technology as well as our *search for truth* has brought us to the very brink of escape from the endless loop of "evolve and destroy."

We've done many things necessary to set the stage for the next generation, and it is up to them to grab the baton and run. If they can find a way to bring consciousness to a critical mass of the Earth's human population, the tide will be turned, and this beautiful planet will harbor peace and universal love in unprecedented proportions—a goal whose premise involves no mystery. That, perhaps, is our one true mission: to ultimately live in eternal peace and harmony. Maybe *that* is what a soul is, energy of the purest and highest vibration—peace and harmony. And to develop such a soul takes time and work.

Our drive toward this development seems unstoppable, even when you consider the adversity that must be overcome. Burgeoning populations and the resultant societal problems seem overwhelming, and yet the great wave of consciousness rolling across the planet grows and grows. That growth, combined with our stunning technological advance, underscores the hope for our mission. This new generation—the Indigo Children—possesses the confidence and single-mindedness about its mission to get the job done. It's almost as if it comes into the world *knowing* its mission.

This new generation has a different attitude, to be sure, but you must allow your frustration to be tempered with the realization that *they* will be the ones who save the world from itself. We couldn't finish the job, but they can. *They* come with no baggage, no ties to the struggles of their ancestors, no emotional scars. They are born clearly knowing their mission. All they need from us is unconditional love, a vote of confidence, and *choices*. If we offer them choices, they will make the right selections.

Mind, Body, Spirit: Some Final Words

As you read and finish this book and suggested readings, especially Candace Pert's *Molecules of Emotion,* you will come to see that the mind and the body are one. The mind is a higher part of the body, a finer part—*much* less dense—and it is capable of totally directing the actions of the physical body. The *physical body* means the part of the body that we regard as *matter*—that is, of a form of matter that is dense enough for the human senses to observe and feel.

But this thinking apparatus that we call the "mind" seems to be more than just chemicals put together in a certain way. It seems to have a unique feature that we refer to as *consciousness*, and with it a *will*. We are the only animal capable of lying—but we are also the only animal capable of "working on" itself. These features apparently make us unique to our known universe.

We work on ourselves by going through life separating the fine from the coarse; upgrading energies; transforming, through our consciousness and will, the foods that feed our three main centers: food, air, and impressions. As we do this consistently and consciously, we draw a blueprint for our body to follow, and it *will* follow. If we do not consciously work on ourselves in this manner, then the body is completely at the mercy of outside influence, subject to and directed by the law of accident. It becomes a machine with no direction or instruction, and responds to whatever external conditions affect it.

This is why people who do not consciously work on themselves view "zone" experiences as random events—because they are. They occasionally *accidentally* upgrade a certain energy, causing a *brief alignment* of factors (hence the stumbling into the zone), but quickly exit that state as the alignment fades. But when you are constantly *consciously working* at upgrading energies, you are at the same time cultivating these alignments, always shaping them into higher forms, and the body responds efficiently and specifically.

The "tighter" the alignments, the more direct the body's response. It operates through feedback, and it is vital that the feedback is clear, objective, and strong.

Impressions alone, and using only sensual feedback to act, are not enough. The impressions must be passed through our *consciousness*—siphoned through our transmuting station— and then transmitted to the physical body. Only then can the body act with clear instruction, impervious to random external influence.

It is the real aim of this book that, by learning to work on your three main centers simultaneously, you will take control of your "machine," and your life. And that you will begin to elevate your every performance, whether that performance is on a golf course or tennis court, in a boardroom or office, in a classroom or your home, or in any other facet of your life. Upgrading energies is applicable to every second of your life, in everything that you do.

Another aim of this work is that you will, by example and through the sharing of knowledge, influence others—especially the children—to begin to work on themselves. You can be instrumental in helping humanity reach that critical mass and break free from the endless loop that at present seems to be spiraling downward. Imagine a world where everyone is constantly upgrading energies, transmuting negative emotions, and separating the fine from the coarse, in all that they do.

It can easily happen, if you hold that vision and create the intention. *You* have the power to do that. It must begin with you.

Try to remember that we, as humans, are unique. We eat impressions and excrete behavior. *But unlike any other living thing, we can control the digestion.*

God, in His mercy, has given us the gift.

Above all, you must remember something my friend Tony Schueler has said, as often as you can: *"We hold in our hands the body of our Being."* Thanks for that important and timeless quote, Tony.

APPENDIX 1

A Note on Objective Music

Georges Ivanovitch Gurdjieff, aside from being a true master in the realm of psychology and philosophy, was also a composer of music and choreographer of dance. This is not in the usual sense, but in the category of *objective art.*

Gurdjieff counted among his esteemed group of students the famous Russian composer and pianist Thomas De Hartmann, and it was De Hartmann (because of his intimacy with "the work") whom Gurdjieff tapped to become his collaborator in the composition of his music. Gurdjieff created a number of "sacred dances," which were called the *movements,* and these dances, performed within the context of the ancient universal symbol of the enneagram, were designed to include certain gestures and movements that expressed cosmic laws, namely, the Laws of Three and Seven. And the music that was composed to accompany these sacred dances, the *music for the movements,* is not only a remarkable collection but is also the only known truly objective music in existence.

Never before available to the public, the music has, after years of research into private archives and careful production, recently been made available on a very limited basis. I have been fortunate enough to acquire the two-CD set, and I can tell you that after listening to this stunning collection, your life will never be the same. Places in your being are touched that you never knew existed, and no part of you, however hidden or buried, can escape unaffected. Now I know what objective

187

music really is. It is music that you never get a chance to interpret. It simply reaches inside of you, seeks out that part of your being that is its target, and shows it to you objectively, with total openness and honesty. It reveals to you, clearly, your total being. And that is good, because in the process it just rips away layers and layers of the "reel" of ego and personalities that obscures your essence. After my first listening, I just wanted to cry from sheer joy. It's sort of like falling in love, but with *yourself.*

This two-CD set is put out by Channel Crossings Music and is distributed by Channel Classics Records in Herwijnen, Holland. Their fax number, the only contact I have available, is 011-31-418-581-782. As I said, there are very few available. After you've become familiar with Gurdjieff's work, I urge you to attempt to acquire this incredible and unique music.

The Perfect Twosome, Continued

Those of you who are familiar with my second book, *Beyond Golf* (Stillpoint, 1996), will recall chapter 1, titled "The Perfect Twosome." That single chapter, a fictional story within the nonfiction book, elicited more response than anything else that I've ever published. The story seems to touch the heart of anyone who reads it. I get letters, faxes, and phone calls every week from people telling me that the story touched their lives in many positive ways. I was even contacted by the movie industry about the possibility of expanding it into a full-length piece. Considering the popularity of "The Perfect Twosome," I've decided to proceed with its expansion, adding new material until there is enough for the story to stand on its own, and then filling it in to full book length. And in this book, you will get a preview of the continuing work.

Let's pick up on the life and times of Jeffrey Jon Ryan, at the same time remembering that the most important applications of "zone-reaching techniques" lie not in the realm of athletic performance, but in the arena of real-life situations and valued relationships. We must also remember here that the decision to consciously "work on oneself" starts the process of unwinding the "reel of personalities." This effort will bring one closer to one's essence and therefore closer to the zone state.

Jeffrey Jon Ryan, at age forty-five, had been in the throes of a midlife crisis. His marital, professional, and social spheres had crumbled. On a trip to the Monterey Peninsula, taken as a last-ditch effort to regain control and re-ignite the fires, he played a round of golf at storied Pebble Beach, a mystical spot and the scene, through its long history, of many transformational experiences. His round proved to be not only transformational, but magical as well. "Jon" was paired with a youngster in his early teens, and as the magic unfolded and reached a crescendo on the famous eighteenth green, with the ocean pounding and the low, heavy clouds rolling in and obscuring Jon's vision, he learned the true identity of his young, yet intriguingly insightful companion. He was none other than Jon himself, at age fourteen. *Glimpsing* his essence, and getting reacquainted with his innocence, Jon realized an awakening, and his life began to reassemble. But the glimpse, however powerful, proved inadequate in the end, and was not enough to sustain him indefinitely. He needed more, a more lasting, more powerful influence. . . .

Jeffrey Jon Ryan, bearing down on fifty, walked out of the Holt Building into a cold sleet that had just begun. The darkening skies belied the fact that it was only 3 P.M., and the diving temperatures gave promise of the impending snowstorm. It was a far-too-familiar midwinter Chicago afternoon. He raised his collar against the wind and began the four-block walk to his office in the Kepler Center. Despite the distraction of the elements, he tried to digest the contents of his latest "meeting" with Dr. Kenneth Walton, his psychotherapist, former college classmate, and fellow golf-team member.

"Jon," as he was called by his friends and family, trusted Ken Walton like a brother and admired his talent as well as his intellect. For those reasons, he ignored the accepted doctrine of avoiding close friends regarding personal psychological problems. Both men were emotionally and intellectually beyond having to accept such doctrine. They trusted and admired one another completely and were able to compartmentalize their interactions, which took place on several levels. Jon was Ken's "patient," Ken was Jon's client in personal finances, and they were weekend golfing partners as well as social "buddies," families included.

Jon had started "meeting" with Ken Walton as a client/patient a couple of years after his experience at Pebble Beach. That experience had been an "awakening" of sorts for Jon, and his life had taken a decided upturn as a result—at least, for a while. While the experience of glimpsing his essence had been profound, it did not provide the substance for ongoing work. It had been revealing, one of those "good shocks," but its effects, without a backup "practice," were destined to erode with time. But *this* time, at least, he knew enough to seek help. And so one day on the golf course, a place that has a way of laying bare the souls of men, Jon asked Ken Walton for an appointment.

Ken learned of Jon's "experience" during the first visit, and it had been the main topic of discussion during the ensuing weeks and months. This visit had marked six months of weekly visits, and the men had begun to unravel the knots that had formed in the two years following Jon and Debbie's trip to the Monterey Peninsula. While serving as a catalyst to relight the fire of their marriage, the trip (and Jon's experience) had not provided a supply of *fuel,* a supply that could be tapped when needed. When the flame inevitably began to flicker and die, the couple was at a loss to rekindle it.

Ken Walton had been a serious student of the teachings of G. I. Gurdjieff for years, and he knew the system. Gurdjieff, in the view of many of the twentieth century's greatest minds in philosophy and psychology, had the most complete and important cosmology in existence. And Ken knew that Jon's experience at Pebble Beach, as valuable as it was, was incomplete and lacking. He knew *exactly* why the transformational effects of that Pebble Beach experience had worn thin. And in their "sessions" he went about explaining it all to Jon. The first thing that had to be done was to verse Jon in the main basic tenets of the Gurdjieff teachings. Only with this foundation could he possibly understand the steps that would become necessary farther on. And so the teaching had begun.

"Jon," Ken had said, "your experience at Pebble Beach was

just a glimpse, but it served a very important purpose, that is, to begin to awaken you. You were asleep, almost irretrievably. Most people never wake up. As we go along here, you'll understand better the significance of this.

"When we're born, Jon, we emerge into the world as pure awareness, pure *essence. Who and what we are.* No *ego,* no *manifestations,* no *personalities,* no *roles.* Just essence, honest and open. When you marvel at the pure joy of a young child, and for a second share in that joy, it touches a chord in you, the chord of essence that lies buried. It's fleeting. And when you turn away to interact with the 'world of personalities' out there—and the various roles it requires—that 'touch of essence' goes into hiding, until some accidental stylus touches it once again.

"The very young child doesn't know these many personalities, these various roles. He operates only as essence until the ego begins to develop. As the ego develops, various personalities begin to form—manifestations of behavior that fit appropriately (or so we think) to each interaction, each situation. These personalities, as they develop, begin to 'wrap around' our essence, burying it under layer upon layer.

"This 'reel' can become quite extensive and complex, and can, if unchecked and allowed to grow, bury essence to irretrievable depths. The longer a man lives with no attempt at finding and returning to essence, the larger the reel becomes, and the farther the man moves away from his essence. This is what is meant by being 'lost' or 'asleep.'

"But if some life circumstance, some 'shock,' is sufficiently strong, it can cause something of an 'awakening,' which can result in a man 'working on' himself. And if the 'work' is right, a man can begin to work his way back toward essence. He can find himself again, and begin to live in truth. Only then is real freedom realized, for as a man moves away from essence, and begins to live in various 'roles,' he moves away from truth, and lives in lies.

"You made a move toward essence, Jon, two years ago, but

you didn't get close enough. You couldn't, because your glimpse was incomplete. You needed to go back farther, to the time of your *total* essence. That fourteen-year-old that you encountered had already begun to form the 'reel of personalities.' The reel was still small then, but there was enough to *partially* obscure your true essence. Before the real work can begin, you've got to make contact with it. And that's what I'm going to help you do.

"To begin to work on oneself, the first step, following the 'shock' (and the shock can be something quite benign, like reading a book, or 'hearing' something in a conversation), is to awaken. Usually the shock needed is of a less benign nature, like a divorce, death, or financial or personal disaster. Generally, the more asleep a man is, the greater the shock needed to awaken him. But once a man has been shocked into desiring a different direction for his life, he becomes fertile ground for self-work.

"The next step is to begin to 'remember oneself.' This is a vital and important point and must be understood, and all 'right' self-work must begin with this cornerstone. To even begin to 'remember yourself,' you must first realize that you are *two*.

"One, the 'I,' is your true self, your *essence*. And the other is your *ego* and its *many manifestations*, or *personalities*. And the first step is to not only realize this, but to watch, with the 'I,' the parade of personalities as they manifest in different situations.

"You have to constantly keep a 'guardian at the door' and simply observe who comes and goes, the good, the bad, and the ugly. And you just continue to remember to observe. Through this consistent and constant practice of 'remembering yourself,' the 'I,' your essence, grows stronger and begins to become the dominant feature.

"Another aspect of remembering oneself is to realize that the body is a machine. It is imperative that you pay great attention to the machine and learn how it works. For instance, each person repeats a set number of postures and gestures throughout his life. All movement is simply getting from one posture or gesture to another. By observing this consistently repeating process, we learn the intricacies of the machine, and further, by periodically *intentionally* altering these ritualistic positions, we begin to gain mastery over the machine (the physical, or *moving* center) and thereby increase the harmonious interaction between it and the other centers (intellectual, emotional, instinctive, and sexual).

"Jon, that day at Pebble Beach, you began to awaken, and the boy you observed was the manifestation of a side of *you* that had already been buried under years of 'reels.' Yes, you were purer then, and mostly honest, but even so that personality was far from essence. The ego was well formed, and several 'layers' of personality were already in place. The catalyst that caused that experience of awakening was your love for Debbie, and the desperation that you felt at the possibility of losing her. It all provided a sufficient 'shock' that jolted you awake, and the effects caused a momentary move in the right direction.

"But unfortunately you didn't have any reinforcing knowledge to build on and keep it going. So here you are, fearful again, your life once again beginning to deteriorate. But at least you're partially awake and armed with some knowledge of these matters. And next week, Jon, I'm going to lay out a game plan for you, one that I think will enable you to find your *true essence*, continue to live in its complete freedom and its truth, and live your life in peace. To live in peace, with freedom, one must live in truth. And *essence* is *only* capable of truth."

So Jeffrey Jon Ryan walked into his office, shook off the bitter chill, and sat at his desk with a cup of coffee. He felt exhilarated and optimistic after this session. He felt the promise one feels when things take a decided turn for the better. Aside from being a brilliant therapist, Ken Walton had a way of instilling hope in people, and then he followed it up with solid work. He was a *complete* psychologist and psychotherapist—he was well versed in philosophy, possessed a vast range of knowledge, and was a master of the social graces. Jon knew that the next session would be profound, that the analysis was over. And he had no idea what to expect. Ken had asked him to clear his schedule for one complete week, Monday through Monday, beginning the Monday after next Wednesday's appointment, and had given him this one week's notice. And he had told Jon to let Debbie know that he would be away from home for one week, as per Ken's orders. It would all be explained at next week's session, one week from today. . . .

The Ryans' lives in the months following their trip to the Monterey Peninsula had been harmonious. The world had seemed brighter, and for a while everything had seemed like "old times." But it didn't take very long for the hustle and bustle to eclipse the second honeymoon, and to eventually win out over good intention. And once again, due to deadlines, busy schedules, and "striving in general," Jon had unwittingly allowed their personal relationship to begin to erode. Gradually, insidiously, as a result of the neglect, the old hostilities worked their way to the surface. And even though on one level they were periodically aware of what was happening, on another, the level of everyday reality, they seemed powerless to stop the negative momentum.

So one day Jon told Debbie that he was making an appointment with Ken Walton, that he needed expert advice, that his life was out of control. He said that he didn't know whether or not it was possible to recapture the flavor of the "old days"—so much water having passed under the bridge—but that he needed to find out.

Debbie, of course, was happy to see Jon recognizing the need for help, and she thought the world of Ken Walton, but at the same time she felt tired and beaten. The illusion that had been created in California had long faded, and she doubted Jon's ability to change for the long term. As long as his work totally consumed him, as long as he felt so *driven* to get *more*, she felt that their marriage had run its course. Jon's passion for his work was fine and good, but in his case it exhausted *all* of his passion. They had no mutual interest. They not only didn't know how to "play" together anymore, they had *nothing to play*.

For a long time after their marriage, Jon had always had some of the "little boy," the playfulness, in him. And that part of him had kept the marriage fun even in tough times. But that little boy had gotten lost along the way, and had long been gone. He reappeared briefly in Monterey, but then had soon again vanished. Without that little boy part of him, Jon was just an empty shell of his former self, just like their marriage.

So even though Debbie applauded Jon's reaching out, she remained naturally skeptical. She'd now watched two honeymoons fade away into the sunset, and didn't relish getting set up for another fall. Besides, she'd settled into a life of her own, with her own interests and her own friends, and at this point in her life it almost seemed enough. Almost—but from a distance, she decided to watch and secretly hope. While Jon was going through therapy, she decided to hit the pause button.

Meanwhile, Jon had learned a great deal from Ken. He'd learned a great deal about himself and, by virtue of his indoctrination in the teachings of G. I. Gurdjieff, about life and the world in general. So with all of this positive momentum, and the "blueprint" promised by Ken, he finally felt excitement about the possibilities for the future. And on that Wednesday, sitting at his desk ignoring the stack of messages before him, he called Debbie to tell her that they had dinner reservations at Charlie Trotters, their favorite restaurant. It meant a special occasion. The reservations are for eight o'clock, he'd said, *for two.*

The enthusiasm in Jon's voice had sent Debbie scurrying to the closet, and she'd spent a considerable amount of time picking out the "right" outfit. Something must be up, she said to herself, because dinner at Charlie Trotters is no everyday occasion. Dinner *there,* in itself, is an extraordinary experience—very expensive, very romantic, *very* good. There were no business dinners there; it was a place that had been, through the years, their very own secret, their personal, private conference room.

They arrived at the restaurant at 7:45 and had martinis at the bar and made small talk. It was their typical ritualistic prelude—their way of building up to the important stuff. Fifteen minutes later, Jon and Debbie were led to their table and seated, and they were perusing the wine list. Jon selected a 1994 Clos Du Bois Merlot, an exceptionally smooth and flavorful vintage. With its pouring came a toast, to the future and to their health and happiness, and it all gave Jon the courage and impetus to launch into his intended speech.

"Debbie," he said, "you know that I love you, and I know that you love me, and I think that we both want to be happy, with each other. But I also think that somehow, over the years, life has insidiously shifted our focus. At first, like all new lovers, we were consumed with each other. But as time and life with its inevitable chaos go on, people tend to get consumed with other matters, and act as if their love is something *automatic*. Little things between people, the things that at first serve as the glue that keeps them connected, get pushed aside to make room for 'more important' matters—as if any *thing* is more important than their bond. And when enough of these 'important matters' replace the little things, that bond doesn't weaken, but it gets buried, obscured, and can become very hard to find again, unless you are willing to dig down beneath life's rubble and find it. For six months now, with Ken Walton's help, I've been digging. And now I know why the glow of Pebble Beach didn't last. When it faded, I think that both of us were scared that perhaps our run was over, that there wasn't enough left to sustain us. But that's not the case at all. Very simply, we just didn't know *how* to sustain it."

Dinner at Trotters is an event, with all sorts of preliminary courses: sauces, sorbets, more sauces, and several exotic and delicious appetizers. The food, and the presentation, is world class. So far, Jon's monologue had carried them through the salad, and the lamb (racks, fresh from New Zealand) was being served. As the fresh mint jelly was being spooned onto their plates, Jon continued.

He explained to Debbie about *essence* versus the many personalities, about "remembering oneself," and about self-observation. And he said, "The fact is, Debbie, that I'd gotten *so far away* from my essence, that I couldn't find my way back. The glimpse that I got in California was incomplete, and not enough—not *deep* enough—to sustain me. And in the process, as a result, our marriage had gotten away from *its* essence. The 'reel' can get pretty thick, you know, and the center can become indistinguishable and elusive. At next Wednesday's session, Ken is going to give me a game plan, a map, to find my way back to true essence. He told me to completely clear my schedule beginning the Monday after that session, through the following Monday. He told me to tell you that I would be gone for one week, as per his orders. I have no idea what he's going to say, or what he has in store for me, but he said that it will be profound, that I will return to essence. And he says that even more importantly, I'll learn how to live, every day, in its freedom and its truth. And Debbie, I feel that by regaining control over *my* life, we can regain control of *our* lives, and recapture the essence of our love."

Through all of Jon's sincere and eloquent "speech," Debbie had sat silently and listened attentively. This sounds like the old Jon, she'd thought to herself, the one who'd courted her and won her heart so long ago. But at the same time she was reluctant to allow herself to be seduced by the charm. She'd made that mistake once before. So she decided to just wait and see, to keep an open mind. She was curious to see what Ken had in mind for her good but beleaguered man.

After a perfect dessert and a glass of Cles De Duc Armagnac, dinner officially ended. The Ryans left the restaurant and headed home with satisfied stomachs and hopeful hearts. The forty-five-minute drive home to the suburbs was filled with flirting, teasing, and sexual innuendo. And it carried on into the bedroom, where their passion exploded. It had been a long dry spell.

The next few days were pleasant, peaceful, yet exciting ones.

And suddenly it was Wednesday. Jon arrived at the Holt Building five minutes early, signed in, and took a seat in the waiting room. The receptionist soon slid open the glass partition and, just as she'd done for the last six months, told Jon that he could go on in. Ken was incredibly punctual, always organized and prepared. He said that in his field you had to be, or else the resultant anxiety and chaos would transfer to the patient—the last thing that most of the patients needed.

Ken Walton's inner office was an example of taste and understated elegance. It was sort of a very warm and cozy personal library, complete with oversized soft leather chairs, Persian rugs, a fireplace, lots of books in beautiful antique walnut and glass bookcases, a library ladder, and a quaint little inner reading room with its own fireplace and sound system—and wet bar. It was the kind of place that you could stay in forever, womblike in security and comfort. Jon settled into "his" chair, the only one he'd ever used. At his first session with Ken, he'd felt drawn to this particular chair. It faced the fireplace, and to the right was one of the huge bookcases. It was, for Jon, a comfortable spot. After greetings, Ken got right to the point.

"Schedule all clear for next week, Jon?" he asked.

"Yep," Jon answered. "And Debbie knows that I'll be gone for a week. I think she might even miss me a little, the way the last few days have gone."

"I'm gonna miss you too—gonna miss your money," said Ken, alluding to the fact that on Saturday he'd clipped Jon for a few bucks on the golf course. "So Jon, I'm sure you're wondering where I'm sending you, and what you're going to do. Let's get straight to the point. I'm sending you off to spend a week with little *Jeffie*, with your essence."

"Jeffie" was what Jeffrey Jon Ryan was called as a young child.

"You're going to hang out with Jeffie for a week, and then he's going to come back with you, never to leave again, or rather, never to be *forgotten* by you again. I want you to go to the house you lived in when you were five years old, pick him up, introduce yourself, and go. Then, I want you to retrace your major life steps with him, physically visiting those places that represent important turning points in your life. I want you to relive, *with him,* all the circumstances surrounding those events, and at the same time try to recognize the influences that were acting upon you. In this way, and through an *internal* dialogue with your essence, you can see how the opinions and wishes of your essence were pushed aside in favor of your ego, your 'personality of the moment.' And by connecting once again in a deep and intimate way with your true essence, you will learn to always consult with it on everyday matters—and especially before making important decisions.

"Remember, Jon, that *Jeffie,* who was your essence, operated completely from the heart, from total truth, and from the physical and emotional centers. He did no rationalizing; he played no role. He was *unable* to intellectualize. He did not, of course, have life's experiences to draw from, like you do. But when we combine *your* knowledge of the ways of the world with *his* untainted honesty, what we get is what some call an enlightened being, or a conscious or an awakened soul, or what Gurdjieff referred to as 'man number eighteen.' Your experience and your essence make *the Perfect Twosome.* And we all have this potential pair within us."

Jon, of course, had some questions, so the rest of the session was a discussion of the details of the carrying-out of this exercise. As Ken Walton had said, the dialogue between Jon and Jeffie should be internal, so as to spare Jon the obvious embarrassment of talking to himself in public. Also, there was much discussion about where Jon should go—which places from his past he should visit. These "places" from his past would help facilitate the resurfacing of his essence. There were, of course, the obvious choices like kindergarten, grammar school, high school, college, graduations, marriage, etc., but there turned out to be many other less obvious choices, events that weren't as historically significant and yet were terribly significant on a personal level. So Jon's mission between Wednesday afternoon and Monday morning was to map out an itinerary, and yet to build into it some flexibility, for, after all, who knows where a five-year-old will lead you?

Now back in his office, relaxing at his desk, Jon began to plan his "exercise," and the more he thought about it, the more excited he became. Ken had told him that Jeffie had *always* been with him, every step of the way. But he also told Jon that he had begun to ignore Jeffie more and more as he'd gotten older, as he developed all of these different personalities. These personalities constantly need attention and approval, whereas essence does not, so all essence can do is withdraw from the chaos—let the "personalities" deal with it—and sadly watch the "reel" get larger. Every now and then, when one of the personalities sees something like an incredible sunset, or marvels at a new birth or some other wonder of nature, for one brief introspective moment there is a connection with essence, but that moment is quickly lost as the "noise" of life resumes, a noise that calls forth once again the inevitable "parade of personalities."

Taking out a yellow legal pad, Jon buzzed his secretary, told her to screen out all calls except from Debbie, and began to sketch out an itinerary for the coming week, a week that would prove to be revealing and transformational in the greatest sense. The coming week would change Jon's life forever.

Jon decided that the first stop would be Ridgewood, the private school in the western suburbs of Chicago where his academic career began. What better way to begin this "trip" than to have Jeffie show *him* where he'd gone to kindergarten? Jeffie could take him through a typical day at Ridgewood, and then the two of them could discuss the day's events over dinner.

Ken had explained to Jon that he had to take great care to make this exercise as realistic as possible, down to the smallest details. It would require creative imagination and clear visualization, which fortunately were two of Jon's strongest assets. Jon decided that he would arrive at 2415 Sonnet Lane, his childhood home, at eight o'clock on Monday morning, to "pick up and meet" Jeffie. He would actually go to the house and wait in the car out front, "meet" Jeffie as he "came out," introduce himself, and away they'd go, for a week together. He had already "called" his (and Jeffie's) parents to explain what was going on. Jon realized, of course, that the itinerary was likely to take sudden and unexpected turns, but he wanted to have a general plan, with definite highlights, so that nothing of great importance was missed.

As Jon's tentative schedule began to take shape, included were events like his first date, his first boyhood fight, highlights from sports activities and special times that he'd shared with his father, such as going fishing or to ball games. There were also sad times, like experiencing the death of his first dog, and overhearing his parents fight. As he went through this regression process, he began to recall experiences that had been out of his consciousness for many years, and he marveled at the ability of the human mind to recall such deeply stored memories. Some were happy, and some were not—family deaths, devastating personal failures, etc. He was quickly becoming aware that many of the events in his life, while seeming on the surface to be rather ordinary, in some cases had had profound effects on him. And it was becoming equally clear that one week would not be enough time to "revisit," with his young companion, these places. So faced with this dilemma, he called Ken for some "telephone counsel."

Ken picked up his personal line and said, "Hi, Jon, I've been wondering how long it would take for you to call. You must be deep into the memories by now, and probably overwhelmed by the number of them." It was as if Ken had read Jon's thoughts.

"Quite frankly, Ken, I'm having a tough time prioritizing these events, and wondering how to fit them all in. It's becoming obvious that I can't 'revisit' them all. So hence this call. What do I do?"

"This was completely expected, Jon, but I had to let you go through this regression on your own, to make sure that you got 'deep' enough, and *complete*. So what I want you to do now is to separate your life into three distinct periods. Period one will be your childhood, from your earliest memories to your sixteenth birthday. Period two will be your 'young man' era, from age sixteen to your twenty-first birthday. And period three will be your time as a man, up to the present. Then from each of those three periods, select two events that qualify as 'defining' experiences or, in your opinion, transformational ones. In doing this, follow your heart, your instincts, your *feelings*. Remember, Jon, what you've learned, that your head is often wrong, because it listens to *ego* (one of your *personalities*), but your heart is never wrong, because it listens to *essence*. This will give you a baseline of six events to work from, and although even *that* plan may get sidetracked some, you'll still have a workable plan. And, Jon, don't worry, you will have plenty of time to reminisce with Jeffie about anything you miss on this trip, because he is going to stay with you even after this next week. He's going to walk beside you, and live within you, forever. You're discarding the 'reel' to rediscover essence."

So, over the next few days, Jon refined his and Jeffie's "itinerary," and the plan began to take shape. The exercise was taking on a life of its own and Jon felt energized by it all. He couldn't wait for Monday to come.

Suggested Reading

The Active Side of Infinity, by Carlos Castaneda

Cleansing the Doors of Perception, by Huston Smith

The Four Witnesses, by Robin Griffith-Jones

The Fourth Way, by P. D. Ouspensky

The High-Performance Mind, by Anna Wise

In Search of the Miraculous: Fragments of an Unknown Teaching, by P. D. Ouspensky

The Indigo Children, by Lee Carroll and Jan Tober

Joshua's Way, by Robert P. Baker

Masters of Wisdom: An Esoteric History of the Spiritual Unfolding of Life on This Planet, by John G. Bennett

Molecules of Emotion: Why You Feel the Way You Feel, by Candace Pert

The Mystery Schools, by Grace F. Knoche

Quotations from G. I. Gurdjieff's Teaching, by M. W. Thring

The Secret of Shambhala, by James Redfield

The Walled Garden of Truth: The Hadiqa of Hakim Sanai, by Hakim Sanai